The Necessity of Atheism (annotated)

by Percy Shelley

CW01497961

There Is No God

This negation must be understood solely to affect a creative Deity. The hypothesis of a pervading Spirit co-eternal with the universe remains unshaken.

A close examination of the validity of the proofs adduced to support any proposition is the only secure way of attaining truth, on the advantages of which it is unnecessary to descant: our knowledge of the existence, of a Deity is a subject of such importance that it cannot be too minutely investigated; in consequence of this conviction we proceed briefly and impartially to examine the proofs which have been adduced. It is necessary first to consider the nature of belief.

When a proposition is offered to the mind, It perceives the agreement or disagreement of the ideas of which it is composed. A perception of their agreement is termed belief. Many obstacles frequently prevent this perception from being immediate; these the mind attempts to remove in order that the perception may be distinct. The mind is active in the investigation in order to perfect the state of perception of the relation which the component ideas of the proposition bear to each, which is passive; the investigation being confused with the perception has induced many falsely to imagine that the mind is active in belief. -- that belief is an act of volition, -- in consequence of which it may be regulated by the mind. Pursuing, continuing this mistake, they have attached a degree of criminality to disbelief; of which, in its nature, it is incapable: it is equally incapable of merit.

Belief, then, is a passion, the strength of which, like every other passion, is in precise proportion to the degrees of excitement.

The degrees of excitement are three.

The senses are the sources of all knowledge to the mind; consequently their evidence claims the strongest assent.

The decision of the mind, founded upon our own experience, derived from these sources, claims the next degree.

The experience of others, which addresses itself to the former one, occupies the lowest degree.

(A graduated scale, on which should be marked the capabilities of propositions to approach to the test of the senses, would be a just barometer of the belief which ought to be attached to them.)

Consequently no testimony can be admitted which is contrary to reason; reason is founded on the evidence of our senses.

Every proof may be referred to one of these three divisions: it is to be considered what arguments we receive from each of them, which should convince us of the existence of a Deity.

1st, The evidence of the senses. If the Deity should appear to us, if he should convince our senses of his existence, this revelation would necessarily command belief. Those to whom the Deity has thus appeared have the strongest possible conviction of his existence. But the God of Theologians is incapable of local visibility.

2d, Reason. It is urged that man knows that whatever is must either have had a beginning, or have existed from all eternity, he also knows that whatever is not eternal must have had a cause. When this reasoning is applied to the universe, it is necessary to prove that it was created: until that is clearly demonstrated we may reasonably suppose that it has endured from all eternity. We must prove design before we can infer a designer. The only idea which we can form of causation is derivable from the constant conjunction of objects, and the consequent inference of one from the other. In a base where two propositions are diametrically opposite, the mind believes that which is least incomprehensible; -- it is easier to suppose that the universe has existed from all eternity than to conceive a being beyond its limits capable of creating it: if the mind sinks beneath the weight of one, is it an alleviation to increase the intolerability of the burthen?

The other argument, which is founded on a Man's knowledge of his own existence, stands thus. A man knows not only that he now is, but that once he was not; consequently there must have been a cause. But our idea of causation is alone derivable from the constant conjunction of objects and the consequent Inference of one from the other; and, reasoning experimentally, we can only infer from effects caused adequate to those effects. But there certainly is a generative power which is effected by certain instruments: we cannot prove that it is inherent in these instruments" nor is the contrary hypothesis capable of demonstration: we admit that the generative power is incomprehensible; but to suppose that the same effect is produced by an eternal, omniscient, omnipotent being leaves the cause in the same obscurity, but renders it more incomprehensible.

3d, Testimony. It is required that testimony should not be contrary to reason. The testimony that the Deity convinces the senses of men of his existence can only be admitted by us, if our mind considers it less probable, that these men should have been deceived than that the Deity should have appeared to them. Our reason can never admit the testimony of men, who not only declare that they were eye-witnesses of miracles, but that the Deity was irrational; for he commanded that he should be believed, he proposed the highest rewards for, faith, eternal punishments for disbelief. We can only command voluntary actions; belief is not an act of volition; the mind is ever passive, or involuntarily active; from this it is evident that we have no sufficient testimony, or rather that testimony is insufficient to prove the being of a God. It has been before shown that it cannot be deduced from reason. They alone, then, who have been convinced by the evidence of the senses can believe it.

Hence it is evident that, having no proofs from either of the three sources of conviction, the mind cannot believe the existence of a creative God: it is also evident that, as belief is a passion of the mind, no degree of criminality is attachable to disbelief; and that they only are reprehensible who neglect to remove the false medium through which their mind views any subject of discussion. Every reflecting mind must acknowledge that there is no proof of the existence of a Deity.

God is an hypothesis, and, as such, stands in need of proof: the onus probandi rests on the theist. Sir Isaac Newton says: Hypotheses non fingo, quicquid enim ex phaenomenis non deducitur hypothesis, vocanda est, et hypothesis vel metaphysicae, vel physicae, vel qualitatum occultarum, seu mechanicae, in philosophia locum non habent. To all proofs of the existence of a creative God apply this valuable rule. We see a variety of bodies possessing a variety of powers: we merely know their effects; we are in a estate of ignorance with respect to their essences and causes. These Newton calls the phenomena of things; but the pride of philosophy is unwilling to admit its ignorance of their causes. From the phenomena, which are the objects of our attempt to infer a cause, which we call God, and gratuitously endow it with all negative and contradictory qualities. From this hypothesis we invent this general name, to conceal our ignorance of causes and essences. The being called God by no means answers with the conditions prescribed by Newton; it bears every mark of a veil woven by philosophical conceit, to hide the ignorance of philosophers even from themselves. They borrow the threads of its texture from the anthropomorphism of the vulgar. Words have been used by sophists for the same purposes, from the occult qualities of the peripatetics to the effuvium of Boyle and the crinities or nebulae of Herschel. God is represented as infinite, eternal, incomprehensible; he is contained under every predicate in non that the logic of ignorance could fabricate. Even his worshippers allow that it is impossible to form any idea of him: they exclaim with the French poet,

Pour dire ce qu'il est, il faut etre lui-meme.

Lord Bacon says that atheism leaves to man reason, philosophy, natural piety, laws, reputation, and everything that can serve to conduct him to virtue; but superstition destroys all these, and erects itself into a tyranny over the understandings of men: hence atheism never disturbs the government, but renders man more clear- sighted, since he sees nothing beyond the boundaries of the present life. -- Bacon's Moral Essays.

The [Beginning here, and to the paragraph ending with Systeme de la Nature," Shelley wrote in French. A free translation has been substituted.] first theology of man made him first fear and adore the elements themselves, the gross and material objects of nature; he next paid homage to the agents controlling the elements, lower genies, heroes or men gifted with great qualities. By force of reflection he sought to simplify things by submitting all nature to a single agent, spirit, or universal soul, which, gave movement to nature and all its branches. Mounting from cause to cause, mortal man has ended by seeing nothing; and it is in this obscurity that he has placed his God; it is in this darksome abyss that his uneasy imagination has always labored to fabricate chimeras, which will continue to afflict him until his knowledge of nature chases these phantoms which he has always so adored.

If we wish to explain our ideas of the Divinity we shall be obliged to admit that, by the word God, man has never been able to designate but the most hidden, the most distant and the most unknown cause of the effects which he saw; he has made use of his word only when the play of natural and known causes ceased to be visible to him; as soon as he lost the thread of these causes, or when his mind could no longer follow the chain, he cut the difficulty and ended his researches by calling God the last of the causes, that is to say, that which is beyond all causes that he knew; thus he but assigned a vague denomination to an unknown cause, at which his laziness or the limits of his knowledge forced him to stop. Every time we say that God is the author of some phenomenon, that signifies that we are ignorant of how such a phenomenon was able to operate by the aid of forces or causes that we know in nature. It is thus that the generality of mankind, whose lot is ignorance, attributes to the Divinity, not only the unusual effects which strike them, but moreover the most simple events, of which the causes are the most simple to understand by whomever is able to study them. In a word, man has always respected unknown causes, surprising effects that his ignorance kept him from unraveling. It was on this debris of nature that man raised the imaginary colossus of the Divinity.

If ignorance of nature gave birth to gods, knowledge of nature is made for their destruction. In proportion as man taught himself, his strength and his resources augmented with his knowledge; science, the arts, industry, furnished him assistance; experience reassured him or procured for him means of resistance to the efforts of many causes which ceased to alarm as soon as they became understood. In a word, his terrors dissipated in the same proportion as his mind became enlightened. The educated man ceases to be superstitious.

It is only by hearsay (by word of mouth passed down from generation to generation) that whole peoples adore the God of their fathers and of their priests: authority, confidence, submission and custom with them take the place of conviction or of proofs: they prostrate themselves and pray, because their fathers taught them to prostrate themselves and pray: but why did their fathers fall on their knees? That is because, in primitive times, their legislators and their guides made it their duty. "Adore and believe," they said, "the gods whom you cannot understand; have confidence in our profound wisdom; we know more than you about Divinity." But why should I come to you? It is because God willed it thus; it is because God will punish you if you dare resist. But this God, is not he, then, the thing in question? However, man has always traveled in this vicious circle; his slothful mind has always made him find it easier to accept the judgment of others. All religious nations are founded solely on authority; all the religions of the world forbid examination and do not want one to reason; authority wants one to believe in God; this God is himself founded only on the authority of a few men who pretend to know him, and to come in his name and announce him on earth. A God made by man undoubtedly has need of man to make himself known to man.

Should it not, then, be for the priests, the inspired, the metaphysicians that should be reserved the conviction of the existence of a God, which they, nevertheless, say is so necessary for all mankind? But Can you find any harmony in the theological opinions of the different inspired ones or thinkers scattered over the earth? They themselves, who make a profession of adoring the same God, are they in Agreement? Are they content with the proofs that their colleagues bring of his existence? Do they subscribe unanimously to the ideas they present on nature, on his conduct, on the manner of understanding his pretended oracles? Is there a country on earth where the science of God is really perfect? Has this science anywhere taken the consistency and uniformity that we the see the science of man assume, even in the most futile crafts, the most despised trades. These words mind immateriality, creation, predestination and grace; this mass of subtle distinctions with which theology to everywhere filled; these so ingenious inventions, imagined by thinkers who have succeeded one another for so many centuries, have only, alas! confused things all the more, and never has man's most necessary science, up to this time acquired the slightest fixity. For thousands of years the lazy dreamers have perpetually relieved one another to meditate on the Divinity, to divine his secret will, to invent the proper hypothesis to develop this important enigma. Their slight success has not discouraged the theological vanity: one always speaks of God: one has his throat cut for God: and this sublime being still remains the most unknown and the most discussed.

Man would have been too happy, if, limiting himself to the visible objects which interested him, he had employed, to perfect his real sciences, his laws, his morals, his education, one-half the efforts he has put into his researches on the Divinity. He would have been still wiser and still more fortunate if he had been satisfied to let his jobless guides quarrel among themselves, sounding depths capable of rendering them dizzy, without himself mixing in their senseless disputes. But it is the essence of ignorance to attach importance to that which it does not understand. Human vanity is so constituted that it stiffens before difficulties. The more an object conceals itself from our eyes, the greater the effort we make to seize it, because it pricks our pride, it excites our curiosity and it appears interesting. In fighting for his God everyone, in fact, fights only for the interests of his own vanity, which, of all the passions produced by the mal-organization of society, is the quickest to take offense, and the most capable of committing the greatest follies.

If, leaving for a moment the annoying idea that theology gives of a capricious God, whose partial and despotic decrees decide the fate of mankind, we wish to fix our eyes only on the pretended goodness, which all men, even trembling before this God, agree is ascribing to him, if we allow him the purpose that is lent him of having worked only for his own glory, of exacting the homage of intelligent beings; of seeking only in his works the well-being of mankind; how reconcile these views and these dispositions with the ignorance truly invincible in which this God, so glorious and so good, leaves the majority of mankind in regard to God himself? If God wishes to be known, cherished, thanked, why does he not show himself under his favorable features to all these intelligent beings by whom he wishes to be loved and adored? Why not manifest himself to the whole earth in an unequivocal manner, much more capable of convincing us than these private revelations which seem to accuse the Divinity of an annoying partiality for some of his creatures? The all-powerful, should he not heave more convincing means by which to show man than these ridiculous metamorphoses, these pretended incarnations, which are attested by writers so little in agreement among themselves? In place of so many miracles, invented to prove the divine mission of so many legislators revered by the different people of the world, the Sovereign of these spirits, could he not convince the human mind in an instant of the things he wished to make known to it? Instead of hanging the sun in the vault of the firmament, instead of scattering stars without order, and the constellations which fill space, would it not have been more in conformity with the views of a God so jealous of his glory and so well-intentioned for mankind, to write, in a manner not subject to dispute, his name, his attributes, his permanent wishes in ineffaceable characters, equally understandable to all the inhabitants of the earth? No one would then be able to doubt the existence of God, of his clear will, of his visible intentions. Under the eyes of this so terrible God no one would have the audacity to violate his commands, no mortal would dare risk attracting his anger: finally, no man would have the effrontery to impose on his name or to interpret his will according to his own fancy.

In fact, even while admitting the existence of the theological God, and the reality of his so discordant attributes which they impute to him, one can conclude nothing to authorize the conduct or the cult which one is prescribed to render him. Theology is truly the sieve of the Danaides. By dint of contradictory qualities and hazarded assertions it has, that is to say, so handicapped its God that it has made it impossible for him to act. If he is infinitely good, what reason should we have to fear him? If he is infinitely wise, why should we have doubts concerning our future? If he knows all, why warn him of our needs and fatigue him with our prayers? If he is everywhere, why erect temples to him? If he is just, why fear that he will punish the creatures that he has, filled with weaknesses? If grace does everything for them, what reason would he have for recompensing them? If he is all-powerful, how offend him, how resist him? If he is reasonable, how can he be angry at the blind, to whom he has given the liberty of being unreasonable? If he is immovable, by what right do we pretend to make him change his decrees? If he is inconceivable, why occupy ourselves with him? IF HE HAS SPOKEN, WHY IS THE UNIVERSE NOT CONVINCED? If the knowledge of a God is the most necessary, why is it not the most evident and the clearest. -- Systame de la Nature. London, 1781.

The enlightened and benevolent Pliny thus Publicly professes himself an atheist, -- Quapropter effigiem Del formamque quaerere imbecillitatis humanae reor. Quisquis est Deus (si modo est alius) et quacunque in parte, totus est gensus, totus est visus, totus auditus, totus animae, totus animi, totus sul. ... Imperfectae vero in homine naturae praecipua solatia, ne deum quidem omnia. Namque nec sibi protest mortem consciscere, si velit, quod homini dedit optimum in tantis vitae poenis; nee mortales aeternitate donare, aut revocare defunctos; nec facere ut qui vixit non vixerit, qui honores gessit non gesserit, nullumque habere In praeteritum ius praeterquam oblivionts, atque (ut. facetis quoque argumentis societas haec cum, deo compuletur) ut bis dena viginti non sint, et multa similiter efficere non posse. -- Per quaedeclaratur haud dubie naturae potentiam id quoque ease quod Deum vocamus. -- Plin. Nat. Hist. cap. de Deo.

The consistent Newtonian is necessarily an atheist. See Sir W. Drummond's Academical Questions, chap. iii. -- Sir W. seems to consider the atheism to which it leads as a sufficient presumption of the falsehood of the system of gravitation; but surely it is more consistent with the good faith of philosophy to admit a deduction from facts than an hypothesis incapable of proof, although it might militate, with the obstinate preconceptions of the mob. Had this author, instead of inveighing against the guilt and absurdity of atheism, demonstrated its falsehood, his conduct would have, been more suited to the modesty of the skeptic and the toleration of the philosopher.

Omnia enim per Dei potentiam facta aunt: imo quia naturae potentia nulla est nisi ipsa Dei potentia. Certum est nos eatenus Dei potentiam non intelligere, quatenus causas naturales ignoramus; adeoque stulte ad eandem Dei potentism recurritur, quando rei alicuius causam naturalem, sive est, ipsam Dei potentiam ignoramusd -- Spinoza, Tract. Theologico-Pol. chap 1. P. 14.

On Life

Life and the world, or whatever we call that which we are and feel, is an astonishing thing. The mist of familiarity obscures from us the wonder of our being. We are struck with admiration at some of its transient modifications, but it is itself the great miracle. What are changes of empires, the wreck of dynasties, with the opinions which support them; what is the birth and the extinction of religious and of political systems, to life? What are the revolutions of the globe which we inhabit, and the operations of the elements of which it is composed, compared with life? What is the universe of stars, and suns, of which this inhabited earth is one, and their motions, and their destiny, compared with life? Life, the great miracle, we admire not because it is so miraculous. It is well that we are thus shielded by the familiarity of what is at once so certain and so unfathomable, from an astonishment which would otherwise absorb and overawe the functions of that which is its object.

If any artist, I do not say had executed, but had merely conceived in his mind the system of the sun, and the stars, and planets, they not existing, and had painted to us in words, or upon canvas, the spectacle now afforded by the nightly cope of heaven, and illustrated it by the wisdom of astronomy, great would be our admiration. Or had he imagined the scenery of this earth, the mountains, the seas, and the rivers; the grass, and the flowers, and the variety of the forms and masses of the leaves of the woods, and the colors which attend the setting and the rising sun, and the hues of the atmosphere, turbid or serene, these things not before existing, truly we should have been astonished, and it would not have been a vain boast to have said of such a man, "Non merita nome di creatore, se non Iddio ed il Poeta." But how these things are looked on with little wonder, and to be conscious of them with intense delight is esteemed to be the distinguishing mark of a refined and extraordinary person. The multitude of men care not for them. It is thus with Life -- that which includes all.

What is life? Thoughts and feelings arise, with or without, our will, and we employ words to express them. We are born, and our birth is unremembered, and our infancy remembered but in fragments; we live on, and in living we lose the apprehension of life. How vain is it to think that words can penetrate the mystery of our being! Rightly used they may make evident our ignorance to ourselves; and this is much. For what are we? Whence do we come? and whither do we go? Is birth the commencement, is death the conclusion of our being? What is birth and death?

The most refined abstractions of logic conduct to a view of life, which, though startling to the apprehension, is, in fact, that which the habitual sense of its repeated combinations has extinguished in us. It strips, as it were, the painted curtain from this scene of things. I confess that I am one of those who am unable to refuse my assent to the conclusion of those philosophers who assert that nothing exists but as it is perceived.

It is a decision against which all our persuasions struggle, and we must be long convicted before we can be convinced that the solid universe of external things is "such stuff as dreams are made of." The shocking absurdities of the popular philosophy of mind and matter, its fatal consequences in morals, and their violent dogmatism concerning the source of all things, had early conducted me to materialism. This materialism is a seducing system to young and superficial minds. It allows its disciples to talk, and dispenses them from thinking. But I was discontented with such a view of things as it afforded; man is a being of high aspirations, "looking both before and after," whose "thoughts wander through eternity," disclaiming alliance with transience and decay: incapable of imagining to himself annihilation; existing but in the future and the past; being, not what he is, but what he has been and all be. Whatever may be his true and final destination, there is a spirit within him at enmity with nothingness and dissolution. This is the character of all life and being. Each is at once the center and the circumference; the point to which all things are referred, and the line in which all things are contained. Such contemplations as these, materialism and the popular philosophy of mind and matter alike they are only consistent with the intellectual system.

It is absurd to enter into a long recapitulation of arguments sufficiently familiar to those inquiring minds, whom alone a writer on abstruse subjects can be conceived to address. Perhaps the most clear and vigorous statement of the intellectual system is to be found in Sir William Drummond's Academical Questions. After such an exposition, it would be idle to translate into other words what could only lose its energy and fitness by the change. Examined point by point, and word by word, the most discriminating intellects have been able to discern no train of thoughts in the process of reasoning, which does not conduct inevitably to the conclusion which has been stated.

What follows from the admission? It establishes no new truth, it gives us no additional insight into our hidden nature, neither its action nor itself: Philosophy, impatient as it may be to build, has much work yet remaining as pioneer for the overgrowth of ages. it makes one step towards this object; it destroys error, and the roots of error. It leaves, what it is too often the duty of the reformer in political and ethical questions to leave, a vacancy. it reduces the mind to that freedom in which it would have acted, but for the misuse of words and signs, the instruments of its own creation. By signs, I would be understood in a wide sense, including what is properly meant by that term, and what I peculiarly mean. In this latter sense, almost all familiar objects are signs, standing, not for themselves, but for others, in their capacity of suggesting one thought which shall lead to a train of thoughts. Our whole life is thus an education of error.

Let us recollect our sensations as children. What a distinct and intense apprehension had we of the world and of ourselves! Many of the Circumstances of social life were then important to us which are now no longer so. But that is not the point of comparison on which I mean to insist. We less habitually distinguished all that we saw and felt, from ourselves. They seemed, as it were, to constitute one mass. There are some persons who, in this respect, are always children. Those who are subject to the state called reverie, feel as if their nature were dissolved into the surrounding universe, or as if the surrounding universe were absorbed into their being. They are conscious of no distinction. And these are states which precede, or accompany, or follow an unusually intense and vivid apprehension of life. As men grow up this power commonly decays, and they become mechanical and habitual agents. Thus feelings and then reasoning are the combined result of a multitude of entangled thoughts, and of a series of what are called impressions, planted by reiteration.

The view of life presented by the most refined deductions of the intellectual philosophy, to that of unity. Nothing exists but as it is perceived. The difference is merely nominal between those two classes of thought which are distinguished by the names of ideas and of external objects. Pursuing the same thread of reasoning, the existence of distinct individual minds, similar to that which is employed in now questioning its own nature, is likewise found to be a delusion. The words, I, you, they, are not signs of any actual difference subsisting between the assemblage of thoughts thus indicated, but are merely marks employed to denote the different modifications of the one mind.

Let it not be supposed that this doctrine conducts the monstrous presumption that I, the person who now write and think, am that one mind. I am but a portion of it. The words I, and you, and they are grammatical devices invented simply for arrangement, and totally devoid of the intense and exclusive sense usually attached to them. It is difficult to find terms adequate to express so subtle a conception as that to which the Intellectual Philosophy has conducted us. We are on that verge where words abandon us, and what wonder if we grow dizzy to look down the dark abyss of how little we know!

The relations of things remain unchanged, by whatever system. By the word things is to be understood any object of thought, that is, any thought upon which any other thought is employed, with an apprehension of distinction. The relations of these remain unchanged; and such is the material of our knowledge.

What is the cause of life? That is, how was it produced, or what agencies distinct from life have acted or act upon life? All recorded generations of mankind have wearily busied themselves in inventing answers to this question; and the result has been -- Religion. Yet that the basis of all things cannot be, as the popular philosophy alleges, mind, is sufficiently evident. Mind, as far as we have any experience of its properties -- and beyond that experience how vain is argument! -- cannot create, it can only perceive. It is said also to be the cause. But cause is only a word expressing a certain state of the human mind with regard to the manner in which two thoughts are apprehended to be related to each other. If anyone desires to know how unsatisfactorily the popular philosophy employs itself upon this great question, they need only impartially reflect upon the manner in which thoughts develop themselves in their minds. It is infinitely improbable that the cause of mind, that is, of existence, is similar to mind.

On A Future State

It has been the persuasion of an immense majority of human beings in all ages and nations that we continue to live after death -- that apparent termination of all the functions of sensitive and intellectual existence. Nor has mankind been contented with supposing that species of existence which some philosophers have asserted; namely, the resolution of the component parts of the mechanism of a living being into its elements, and the impossibility of the minutest particle of these sustaining the smallest diminution. They have clung to the idea that sensibility and thought, which they have distinguished from the objects of it, under the several names of spirit and matter, is, in its own nature, less susceptible of division and decay, and that, when the body is resolved into its elements, the principle which animated it will remain perpetual and unchanged. Some philosophers -- and those to whom we are indebted for the most stupendous discoveries in physical science -- suppose, on the other hand, that intelligence is the mere result of certain combinations among the particles of its objects; and those among them who believe that we live after death, recur to the interposition of a supernatural power, which shall overcome the tendency inherent in all material combinations, to dissipate and be absorbed into other forms.

Let us trace the reasoning which in one and the other have conducted to these two opinions, and endeavor to discover what we ought to think on a question of such momentous interest. Let us analyze the ideas and feelings which constitute the contending beliefs, and watchfully establish a discrimination between words and thoughts. Let us bring the question to the test of experience and fact; and ask ourselves, considering our nature in its entire extent, what light we derive from a sustained and comprehensive view of its component parts, which may enable us to assert, with certainty,, that we do or do not live after death.

The examination of this subject requires that it should be stripped of all those accessory topics which adhere to it in the common opinion of men. The existence of a God, and a future state of rewards and punishments are totally foreign to the subject. If it be proved that the world is ruled by a Divine Power, no inference necessarily can be drawn from that circumstance in favor of a future state. It has been asserted, indeed, that as goodness and justice are to be numbered among the attributes of the Deity, he will undoubtedly compensate the virtuous who suffer during life, and that he will make every sensitive being, who does not deserve punishment, happy forever. But this view of the subject, which it would be tedious as well as superfluous to develop and expose, satisfies no person, and cuts the knot which we now seek to untie. Moreover, should it be proved, on the other hand, that the mysterious principle which regulates the proceedings of the universe, to neither intelligent nor sensitive, yet it is not an inconsistency to suppose at the same time, that the animating power survives the body which it has animated, by laws as independent of any supernatural agent as those through which it first became united with it. Nor, if a future state be clearly proved, does it follow that it will be a state of punishment or reward.

By the word death, we express that condition in which natures resembling ourselves apparently cease to be that which they are. We no longer hear them speak, nor see them move. If they have sensations and apprehensions, we no longer participate in them. We know no more than that those external organs, and all that fine texture of material frame, without which we have no experience that life or thought can subsist, are dissolved and scattered abroad. The body is placed under the earth, and after a certain period there remains no vestige even of its form. This is that contemplation of inexhaustible melancholy, whose shadow eclipses the brightness of the world. The common observer is struck with dejection of the spectacle. He contends in vain against the persuasion of the grave, that the dead indeed cease to be. The corpse at his feet is prophetic of his own destiny. Those who have preceded him, and whose voice was delightful to his ear; whose touch met his like sweet and subtle fire: whose aspect spread a visionary light upon his path -- these he cannot meet again. The organs of sense are destroyed, and the intellectual operations dependent on them have perished with their sources. How can a corpse see or feel? its eyes are eaten out, and its heart is black and without motion. What intercourse can two heaps of putrid Clay and crumbling bones hold together? When you can discover where the fresh colors of the faded flower abide, or the music of the broken lyre seek life among the dead. Such are the anxious and fearful contemplations of the common observer, though the popular religion often prevents him from confessing them even to himself.

The natural philosopher, in addition to the sensations common to all men inspired by the event of death, believes that he sees with more certainty that it is attended with the annihilation of sentiment and thought. He observes the mental powers increase and fade with those of the body, and even accommodate themselves to the most transitory changes of our physical nature. Sleep suspends many of the faculties of the vital and intellectual principle; drunkenness and disease will either temporarily or permanently derange them. Madness or idiocy may utterly extinguish the most excellent and delicate of those powers. In old age the mind gradually withers; and as it grew and was strengthened with the body, so does it together with the body sink into decrepitude. Assuredly these are convincing evidences that so soon as the organs of the body are subjected to the laws of inanimate matter, sensation, and perception, and apprehension, are at an end. It is probable that what we call thought is not an actual being, but no more than the relation between certain parts of that infinitely varied mass, of which the rest of the universe is composed, and which ceases to exist so soon as those parts change their position with regard to each other. Thus color, and sound, and taste, and odor exist only relatively. But let thought be considered only as some peculiar substance, which permeates, and is the cause of, the animation of living beings. Why should that substance be assumed to be something essentially distinct from all others, and exempt from subjection to those laws from which no other substance is exempt? It differs, indeed, from all other substances, as electricity, and light, and magnetism, and the constituent parts of air and earth, severally differ from all others. Each of these is subject to change and decay, and to conversion into other forms. Yet the difference between light and earth is scarcely greater than that which exists between life, or thought, and fire. The difference between the two former was never alleged as an argument for eternal permanence of either, in that form under which they first might offer themselves to our notice. Why should the difference between the two latter substances be an argument for the prolongation of the existence of one and not the other, when the existence of both has arrived at their apparent termination? To say that fire exists without manifesting any of the properties of fire, such as light, heat, etc., or that the Principle of life exists without consciousness, or memory, or desire, or motive, is to resign, by an awkward distortion of language, the affirmative of the dispute. To say that the principle of life may exist in distribution among various forms, is to assert what cannot be proved to be either true or false, but which, were it true, annihilates all hope of existence after death, in any sense in which that event can belong to the hopes and fears of men. Suppose, however, that the intellectual and vital principle differs in the most marked and essential manner from all other known substances; that they have all some resemblance between themselves which it in no degree participates. In what manner can this concession be made an argument for its imperishabillity? All that we see or know perishes and is changed. Life and thought differ indeed from everything else. But that it survives that period, beyond which we have no experience of its existence, such distinction and dissimilarity affords no shadow of proof, and nothing but our own desires could have led us to conjecture or imagine.

Have we existed before birth? It is difficult to conceive the possibility of this. There is, in the generative principle of each animal and plant, a power which converts the substances homogeneous with itself. That is, the relations between certain elementary particles of matter undergo a change, and submit to new combinations. For when we use words: principle, power, cause, etc., we mean to express no real being, but only to class under those terms a certain series of coexisting phenomena; but let it be supposed that this principle is a certain substance which escapes the observation of the chemist and anatomist. It certainly may be; thought it is sufficiently unphilosophical to allege the possibility of an opinion as a proof of its truth. Does it see, hear, feel, before its combination with those organs on which sensation depends? Does it reason, imagine, apprehend, without those ideas which sensation alone can communicate? If we have not existed before birth; If, at the period when the parts of our nature on which thought and life depend, seem to be woven together; If there are no reasons to suppose that we have existed before that period at which our existence apparently commences, then there are no grounds for supposing that we shall continue to exist after our existence has apparently ceased. So far as thought and life is concerned, the same will take place with regard to us, individually considered, after death, as had taken place before our birth.

It is said that it is possible that we should continue to exist in some mode totally inconceivable to us at present. This is a most unreasonable presumption. It casts on the adherents of annihilation the burden of proving the negative of a question, the affirmative of which is not supported by a single argument, and which, by its very nature, lies beyond the experience of the human understanding. It is sufficiently easy. indeed, to form any proposition, concerning which we are ignorant, just not so absurd as not to be contradictory in itself, and defy refutation. The possibility of whatever enters into the wildest imagination to conceive is thus triumphantly vindicated. But it is enough that such assertions should be either contradictory to the known laws of nature, or exceed the limits of our experience, that their fallacy or irrelevancy to our consideration should be demonstrated. They persuade, indeed, only those who desire to be persuaded.

This desire to be forever as we are; the reluctance to a violent and unexperienced change, which is common to all the animated and inanimate combinations of the universe, is, indeed, the secret persuasion which has given birth to the opinions of a future state.

Percy Bysshe Shelley

Percy Bysshe Shelley (4 August 1792 – 8 July 1822) was one of the major English Romantic poets, and is regarded by some as among the finest lyric, as well as epic, poets in the English language. A radical in his poetry as well as in his political and social views, Shelley did not see fame during his lifetime, but recognition for his poetry grew steadily following his death. Shelley was a key member of a close circle of visionary poets and writers that included Lord Byron; Leigh Hunt; Thomas Love Peacock; and his own second wife, Mary Shelley, the author of Frankenstein.

Shelley is perhaps best known for such classic poems as Ozymandias, Ode to the West Wind, To a Skylark, Music, When Soft Voices Die, The Cloud and The Masque of Anarchy. His other major works include a groundbreaking verse drama The Cenci (1819) and long, visionary poems such as Queen Mab (later reworked as The Daemon of the World), Alastor, The Revolt of Islam, Adonaïs, Prometheus Unbound (1820)—widely considered to be his masterpiece,— Hellas: A Lyrical Drama (1821), and his final, unfinished work, The Triumph of Life (1822).

Shelley's close circle of friends included some of the most important progressive thinkers of the day, including his father-in-law, the philosopher William Godwin and Leigh Hunt. Though Shelley's poetry and prose output remained steady throughout his life, most publishers and journals declined to publish his work for fear of being arrested for either blasphemy or sedition. Shelley's poetry sometimes had only an underground readership during his day, but his poetic achievements are widely recognized today, and his advanced political and social thought impacted the Chartist and other movements in England, and reach down to the present day. Shelley's theories of economics and morality, for example, had a profound influence on Karl Marx; his early—perhaps first—writings on nonviolent resistance influenced both Leo Tolstoy and Mahatma Gandhi.

Shelley became a lodestone to the subsequent three or four generations of poets, including important Victorian and Pre-Raphaelite poets such as Robert Browning and Dante Gabriel Rossetti. He was admired by Oscar Wilde, Thomas Hardy, George Bernard Shaw, Bertrand Russell, W. B. Yeats, Upton Sinclair and Isadora Duncan.[3] Henry David Thoreau's civil disobedience was apparently influenced by Shelley's non-violence in protest and political action.

Shelley's popularity and influence has continued to grow in contemporary poetry circles.

Shelley was born 4 August 1792 at Field Place, Broadbridge Heath, near Horsham, West Sussex, England. He was the eldest legitimate son of Sir Timothy Shelley, a Whig Member of Parliament for Horsham from 1790–92 and for Shoreham between 1806–12, and his wife, Elizabeth Pilford, a Sussex landowner. He had four younger sisters and one much younger brother. He received his early education at home, tutored by the Reverend Evan Edwards of nearby Warnham. His cousin and lifelong friend Thomas Medwin, who lived nearby, recounted his early childhood in his The Life of Percy Bysshe Shelley. It was a happy and contented childhood spent largely in country pursuits such as fishing and hunting.[4]

In 1802, he entered the Syon House Academy of Brentford, Middlesex. In 1804, Shelley entered Eton College, where he fared poorly, and was subjected to an almost daily mob torment at around noon by older boys, who aptly called these incidents "Shelley-baits". Surrounded, the young Shelley would have his books torn from his hands and his clothes pulled at and torn until he cried out madly in his high-pitched "cracked soprano" of a voice.[5] This daily misery could be attributed to Shelley's refusal to take part in fagging and his indifference towards games and other youthful activities. Because of these peculiarities he acquired the nickname "Mad Shelley".[6] Shelley possessed a keen interest in science at Eton, which he would often apply to cause a surprising amount of mischief for a boy considered to be so sensible. Shelley would often use a frictional electric machine to charge the door handle of his room, much to the amusement of his friends. His friends were particularly amused when his gentlemanly tutor, Mr Bethell, in attempting to enter his room, was alarmed at the noise of the electric shocks, despite Shelley's dutiful protestations.[7] His mischievous side was again demonstrated by "his last bit of naughtiness at school",[6] which was to blow up a tree on Eton's South Meadow with gunpowder. Despite these jocular incidents, a contemporary of Shelley, W.H. Merie, recalls that Shelley made no friends at Eton, although he did seek a kindred spirit without success.

On 10 April 1810, he matriculated at University College, Oxford. Legend has it that Shelley attended only one lecture while at Oxford, but frequently read sixteen hours a day. His first publication was a Gothic novel, Zastrozzi (1810), in which he vented his early atheistic worldview through the villain Zastrozzi; this was followed at the end of the year by St. Irvyne; or, The Rosicrucian: A Romance (dated 1811).[8] In the same year, Shelley, together with his sister Elizabeth, published Original Poetry by Victor and Cazire and, while at Oxford, he issued a collection of verses (ostensibly burlesque but quite subversive), Posthumous Fragments of Margaret Nicholson, with Thomas Jefferson Hogg.

In 1811, Shelley anonymously published a pamphlet called The Necessity of Atheism which was brought to the attention of the university administration and he was called to appear before the College's fellows, including the Dean, George Rowley. His refusal to repudiate the authorship of the pamphlet resulted in his expulsion from Oxford on 25 March 1811, along with Hogg. The rediscovery in mid-2006 of Shelley's long-lost Poetical Essay on the Existing State of Things — a long, strident anti-monarchical and anti-war poem printed in 1811 in London by Crosby and Company as "by a gentleman of the University of Oxford" and dedicated to Harriet Westbrook — gives a new dimension to the expulsion, reinforcing Hogg's implication of political motives ("an affair of party").[9] Shelley was given the choice to be reinstated after his father intervened, on the condition that he would have to recant his avowed views. His refusal to do so led to a falling-out with his father.

Marriage

Four months after being expelled from Oxford, on 28 August 1811, the 19-year-old Shelley eloped to Scotland with the 16-year-old Harriet Westbrook, a pupil at the same boarding school as Shelley's sisters, whom his father had forbidden him to see. Harriet Westbrook had been writing Shelley passionate letters threatening to kill herself because of her unhappiness at the school and at home. Shelley, heartbroken after the failure of his romance with his cousin, Harriet Grove, cut off from his mother and sisters, and convinced he had not long to live, impulsively decided to rescue Harriet Westbrook and make her his beneficiary.[10] Harriet Westbrook's 28-year-old sister Eliza, to whom Harriet was very close, appears to have encouraged the young girl's infatuation with the future baronet.[11] The Westbrooks pretended to disapprove but secretly encouraged the elopement. Sir Timothy Shelley, however, outraged that his son had married beneath him (Harriet's father, though prosperous, had kept a tavern) revoked Shelley's allowance and refused ever to receive the couple at Field Place. Shelley invited his friend Hogg to share his ménage but asked him to leave when Hogg made advances to Harriet. Harriet also insisted that her sister Eliza, whom Shelley detested, live with them. Shelley was also at this time increasingly involved in an intense platonic relationship with Elizabeth Hitchener, a 28-year-old unmarried schoolteacher of advanced views, with whom he had been corresponding. Hitchener, whom Shelley called the "sister of my soul" and "my second self",[12] became his muse and confidante in the writing of his philosophical poem Queen Mab, a Utopian allegory.

During this period, Shelley travelled to Keswick in England's Lake District, where he visited the poet Robert Southey, under the mistaken impression that Southey was still a political radical. Southey, who had himself been expelled from the Westminster School for opposing flogging, was taken with Shelley and predicted great things for him as a poet. He also informed Shelley that William Godwin, author of Political Justice, which had greatly influenced him in his youth, and which Shelley also admired, was still alive.[13] Shelley wrote to Godwin, offering himself as his devoted disciple and informing Godwin that he was "the son of a man of fortune in Sussex" and "heir by entail to an estate of 6,000 £ per an."[14] Godwin, who supported a large family and was chronically penniless, immediately saw in Shelley a source of his financial salvation. He wrote asking for more particulars about Shelley's income and began advising him to reconcile with Sir Timothy.[15] Meanwhile, Sir Timothy's patron, the Duke of Norfolk, a former Catholic who favoured Catholic Emancipation, was also vainly trying to reconcile Sir Timothy and his son, whose political career the Duke wished to encourage.[16] A maternal uncle ultimately supplied money to pay Shelley's debts, but Shelley's relationship with the Duke may have influenced his decision to travel to Ireland.[17] In Dublin, Shelley published his Address to the Irish People, priced at fivepence, "the lowest possible price" to "awaken in the minds of the Irish poor a knowledge of their real state, summarily pointing out the evils of that state and suggesting a rational means of remedy – Catholic Emancipation and a repeal of the Union Act" (the latter "the most successful engine that England ever wielded over the misery of fallen Ireland").[18] His activities earned him the unfavourable attention of the British government.

Shelley was increasingly unhappy in his marriage to Harriet and particularly resented the influence of her older sister Eliza, who discouraged Harriet from breastfeeding their baby daughter (Elizabeth Ianthe Shelley [1813–76]). Shelley accused Harriet of having married him for his money. Craving more intellectual female companionship, he began spending more time away from home, among other things, studying Italian with Cornelia Turner and visiting the home and bookshop of William Godwin. Eliza and Harriet moved back with their parents.

Shelley's mentor Godwin had three highly educated daughters, two of whom, Fanny Imlay and Claire Clairmont, were his adopted step-daughters. Godwin's first wife, the celebrated feminist Mary Wollstonecraft, author of A Vindication of the Rights of Woman, had died giving birth to Godwin's biological daughter Mary Wollstonecraft Godwin, named after her mother. Fanny was the illegitimate daughter of Mary Wollstonecraft and her lover, the diplomat speculator and writer, Gilbert Imlay. Claire was the illegitimate daughter of Godwin's much younger second wife, Mary Jane Clairmont Godwin, whom Shelley considered a vulgar woman – "not a proper person to form the mind of a young girl", he is supposed to have said,[20] and Sir John Lethbridge. The brilliant Mary was being educated in Scotland when Shelley first became acquainted with the Godwin family. When she returned Shelley fell madly in love with her, repeatedly threatening to commit suicide if she didn't return his affections.

On 28 July 1814, Shelley abandoned Harriet, now pregnant with their son

Charles (November 1814 – 1826) and (in imitation of the hero of one of Godwin's novels) he ran away to Switzerland with Mary, then 16, inviting her stepsister Claire Clairmont (also 16) along because she could speak French. The older sister Fanny was left behind, to her great dismay, for she, too, had fallen in love with Shelley. The three sailed to Europe, and made their way across France to Switzerland on foot, reading aloud from the works of Rousseau, Shakespeare, and Mary's mother, Mary Wollstonecraft (an account of their travels was subsequently published by the Shelleys).

After six weeks, homesick and destitute, the three young people returned to England. The enraged William Godwin refused to see them, though he still demanded money, to be given to him under another name, to avoid scandal. In late 1815, while living in a cottage in Bishopsgate, Surrey, with Mary and avoiding creditors, Shelley wrote Alastor, or The Spirit of Solitude. It attracted little attention at the time, but has now come to be recognised as his first major achievement. At this point in his writing career, Shelley was deeply influenced by the poetry of Wordsworth.

Byron

In mid-1816, Shelley and Mary made a second trip to Switzerland. They were prompted to do this by Mary's stepsister Claire Clairmont, who, in competition with her sister, had initiated a liaison with Lord Byron the previous April just before his self-exile on the continent. Byron's interest in her had waned and Claire used the opportunity of introducing him to the Shelleys to act as bait to lure him to Geneva. The Shelleys and Byron rented neighbouring houses on the shores of Lake Geneva. Regular conversation with Byron had an invigorating effect on Shelley's output of poetry. While on a boating tour the two took together, Shelley was inspired to write his Hymn to Intellectual Beauty, often considered his first significant production since Alastor.[21] A tour of Chamonix in the French Alps inspired Mont Blanc, a poem in which Shelley claims to have pondered questions of historical inevitability (determinism) and the relationship between the human mind and external nature. Shelley also encouraged Byron to begin an epic poem on a contemporary subject, advice that resulted in Byron's composition of Don Juan. In 1817, Claire gave birth to a daughter by Byron, Alba, later renamed Allegra, whom Shelley offered to support, making provisions for her and for Claire in his will.

A suicide and a second marriage

After Shelley and Mary's return to England, Fanny Imlay, Mary's half-sister and Claire's stepsister, despondent over her exclusion from the Shelley household and perhaps unhappy at being omitted from Shelley's will, travelled from Godwin's household in London to kill herself in Wales in early October. On 10 December 1816, the body of Shelley's estranged wife Harriet was found in an advanced state of pregnancy[citation needed], drowned in the Serpentine in Hyde Park, London. Shelley had made generous provision for Harriet and their children in his will and had paid her a monthly allowance as had her father. It is thought that Harriet, who had left her children with her sister Eliza and had been living alone under the name of Harriet Smith, mistakenly believed herself to have been abandoned by her new lover, 36-year-old Lieutenant Colonel Christopher Maxwell, who had been deployed abroad, after a landlady refused to forward his letters to her.[22] On 30 December 1816, barely three weeks after Harriet's body was recovered, Shelley and Mary Godwin were married. The marriage was intended partly to help secure Shelley's custody of his children by Harriet and partly to placate Godwin, who had coldly refused to speak to his daughter for two years, and who now received the couple. The courts, however, awarded custody of Shelley and Harriet's children to foster parents, on the grounds that Shelley was an atheist.[23][24]

The Shelleys took up residence in the village of Marlow, Buckinghamshire, where a friend of Percy's, Thomas Love Peacock, lived. Shelley took part in the literary circle that surrounded Leigh Hunt, and during this period he met John Keats. Shelley's major production during this time was Laon and Cythna; or, The Revolution of the Golden City, a long narrative poem in which he attacked religion and featured a pair of incestuous lovers. It was hastily withdrawn after only a few copies were published. It was later edited and reissued as The Revolt of Islam in 1818. Shelley wrote two revolutionary political tracts under the nom de plume, "The Hermit of Marlow." On Boxing Day 1817, presumably prompted by travellers' reports of Belzoni's success (where the French had failed) in removing the 'half sunk and shattered visage' of the so-called 'Young Memnon' from the Ramesseum at Thebes, Shelley and his friend Horace Smith began a poem each about the Memnon or 'Ozymandias,' Diodorus's 'King of Kings' who in an inscription on the base of his statue challenged all comers to 'surpass my works'. Within four months of the publication of Ozymandias (or Rameses II) his seven-and-a-quarter ton bust arrived in London, just too late for Shelley to have seen it.[25]

Italy

Joseph Severn, 1845, Posthumous Portrait of Shelley Writing Prometheus Unbound in Italy.
Early in 1818, the Shelleys and Claire left England to take Claire's daughter, Allegra, to her father Byron, who had taken up residence in Venice. Contact with the older and more established poet encouraged Shelley to write once again. During the latter part of the year, he wrote Julian and Maddalo, a lightly disguised rendering of his boat trips and conversations with Byron in Venice, finishing with a visit to a madhouse. This poem marked the appearance of Shelley's "urbane style". He then began the long verse drama Prometheus Unbound, a re-writing of the lost play by the ancient Greek poet Aeschylus, which features talking mountains and a petulant spirit who overthrows Jupiter. Tragedy struck in 1818 and 1819, when Shelley's son Will died of fever in Rome, and his infant daughter Clara Everina died during yet another household move.

A baby girl, Elena Adelaide Shelley, was born on 27 December 1818 in Naples, Italy and registered there as the daughter of Shelley and a woman named "Marina Padurin". However, the identity of the mother is an unsolved mystery. Some scholars speculate that her true mother was actually Claire Clairmont or Elise Foggi, a nursemaid for the Shelley family. Other scholars postulate that she was a foundling Shelley adopted in hopes of distracting Mary after the deaths of William and Clara.[26] Shelley referred to Elena in letters as his "Neapolitan ward". However, Elena was placed with foster parents a few days after her birth and the Shelley family moved on to yet another Italian city, leaving her behind. Elena died 17 months later, on 10 June 1820.

The Shelleys moved between various Italian cities during these years; in later 1818 they were living in Florence, in a pensione on the Via Valfonda. This street now runs alongside Florence's railway station and the building now on the site, the original having been destroyed in World War II, carries a plaque recording the poet's stay. Here they received two visitors, a Miss Sophia Stacey and her much older travelling companion, Miss Corbet Parry-Jones (to be described by Mary as "an ignorant little Welshwoman"). Sophia had for three years in her youth been ward of the poet's aunt and uncle. The pair moved into the same pensione and stayed for about two months. During this period Mary gave birth to another son; Sophia is credited with suggesting that he be named after the city of his birth, so he became Percy Florence Shelley, later Sir Percy. Shelley also wrote his "Ode to Sophia Stacey" during this time. They then moved to Pisa, largely at the suggestion of its resident Margaret King, who, as a former pupil of Mary Wollstonecraft, took a maternal interest in the younger Mary and her companions. This "no nonsense grande dame"[27] and her common-law husband George William Tighe inspired the poet with "a new-found sense of radicalism". Tighe was an agricultural theorist, and provided the younger man with a great deal of material on chemistry, biology and statistics.[28]

Shelley completed Prometheus Unbound in Rome, and he spent mid-1819 writing a tragedy, The Cenci, in Leghorn (Livorno). In this year, prompted among other causes by the Peterloo Massacre, he wrote his best-known political poems: The Masque of Anarchy and Men of England. These were probably his best-remembered works during the 19th century. Around this time period, he wrote the essay The Philosophical View of Reform, which was his most thorough exposition of his political views to that date.

In 1820, hearing of John Keats's illness from a friend, Shelley wrote him a letter inviting him to join him at his residence at Pisa. Keats replied with hopes of seeing him, but instead, arrangements were made for Keats to travel to Rome with the artist Joseph Severn. Inspired by the death of Keats, in 1821 Shelley wrote the elegy Adonais.

In 1821, Shelley met Edward Ellerker Williams, a British naval officer, and his wife Jane Williams. Shelley developed a very strong affection towards Jane and addressed a number of poems to her. In the poems addressed to Jane, such as With a Guitar, To Jane and One Word is Too Often Profaned, he elevates her to an exalted position worthy of worship.

In 1822, Shelley arranged for Leigh Hunt, the British poet and editor who had been one of his chief supporters in England, to come to Italy with his family. He meant for the three of them — himself, Byron and Hunt — to create a journal, which would be called The Liberal. With Hunt as editor, their controversial writings would be disseminated, and the journal would act as a counter-blast to conservative periodicals such as Blackwood's Magazine and The Quarterly Review.

Leigh Hunt's son, the editor Thornton Leigh Hunt, was later asked by John Bedford Leno whether he preferred Shelley or Byron as a man. He replied:-
"On one occasion I had to fetch or take to Byron some copy for the paper which my father, himself and Shelley, jointly conducted. I found him seated on a lounge feasting himself from a drum of figs. He asked me if I would like a fig. Now, in that, Leno, consists the difference, Shelley would have handed me the drum and allowed me to help myself."[29]

Death

On 8 July 1822, less than a month before his 30th birthday, Shelley drowned in a sudden storm on the Gulf of Spezia while returning from Leghorn (Livorno) to Lerici in his sailing boat, the Don Juan. He was returning from having set up The Liberal with the newly arrived Leigh Hunt. The name Don Juan, a compliment to Byron, was chosen by Edward John Trelawny, a member of the Shelley-Byron Pisan circle. However, according to Mary Shelley's testimony, Shelley changed it to Ariel, which annoyed Byron, who forced the painting of the words "Don Juan" on the mainsail. The vessel, an open boat, was custom-built in Genoa for Shelley. It did not capsize but sank; Mary Shelley declared in her "Note on Poems of 1822" (1839) that the design had a defect and that the boat was never seaworthy. In fact the Don Juan was seaworthy; the sinking was due to a severe storm and poor seamanship of the three men on board.[30]

Some believed his death was not accidental, that Shelley was depressed and wanted to die; others suggest he simply did not know how to navigate. More fantastical theories, including the possibility of pirates mistaking the boat for Byron's, also circulated.[30][31] There is a small amount of material, though scattered and contradictory, suggesting that Shelley may have been murdered for political reasons: previously, at Plas Tan-Yr-Allt, the Regency house he rented at Tremadog, near Porthmadog, north-west Wales, from 1812 to 1813, he had allegedly been surprised and attacked during the night by a man who may have been, according to some later writers, an intelligence agent.[32] Shelley, who was in financial difficulty, left forthwith leaving rent unpaid and without contributing to the fund to support the house owner, William Madocks; this may provide another, more plausible explanation for this story.

In his Recollections of the Last Days of Shelley and Byron, Trelawny noted that the shirt in which Williams's body was clad was "partly drawn over the head, as if the wearer had been in the act of taking it off [. . .] and [he was missing] one boot, indicating also that he had attempted to strip." Trelawny also relates a supposed deathbed confession by an Italian fisherman who claimed to have rammed Shelley's boat to rob him, a plan confounded by the rapid sinking of the vessel.

Shelley's body was washed ashore and later, in keeping with quarantine regulations, was cremated on the beach near Viareggio. In Shelley's pocket was a small book of Keats' poetry, upon hearing this, Byron (never one to give compliments) said of Shelley "I never met a man who wasn't a beast in comparison to him" . The day after the news of his death reached England, the Tory newspaper The Courier gloated: "Shelley, the writer of some infidel poetry, has been drowned, now he knows whether there is God or no."[34] A reclining statue of Shelley's body, depicted as washed up on the shore, created by sculptor Edward Onslow Ford at the behest of Shelley's daughter-in-law, Jane, Lady Shelley, is the centrepiece of the Shelley Memorial at University College, Oxford. An 1889 painting by Louis Édouard Fournier, The Funeral of Shelley (also known as The Cremation of Shelley), contains inaccuracies. In pre-Victorian times it was English custom that women would not attend funerals for health reasons. Mary Shelley did not attend but was featured in the painting, kneeling at the left-hand side. Leigh Hunt stayed in the carriage during the ceremony but is also pictured. Also, Trelawny, in his account of the recovery of Shelley's body, records that "the face and hands, and parts of the body not protected by the dress, were fleshless," and by the time that the party returned to the beach for the cremation, the body was even further decomposed. In his graphic account of the cremation, he writes of Byron being unable to face the scene, and withdrawing to the beach.[35]

Shelley's ashes were interred in the Protestant Cemetery, Rome, near an ancient pyramid in the city walls. His grave bears the Latin inscription, Cor Cordium ("Heart of Hearts"), and, in reference to his death at sea, a few lines of "Ariel's Song" from Shakespeare's The Tempest: "Nothing of him that doth fade / But doth suffer a sea-change / Into something rich and strange." The grave site is the second in the cemetery. Some weeks after Shelley's ashes had been buried, Trelawny had come to Rome, had not liked his friend's position among a number of other graves, and had purchased what seemed to him a better plot near the old wall. The ashes were exhumed and moved to their present location. Trelawny had purchased the adjacent plot, and over sixty years later his remains were placed there.

A memorial was eventually created for Shelley at the Poets' Corner at

Westminster Abbey, along with his old friends Lord Byron and John Keats.

Shelley's heart

Shelley's widow Mary bought a cliff-top home at Boscombe, Bournemouth in 1851. She intended to live there with her son, Percy, and his wife Jane, and had the remains of her own parents moved from their London burial place at St Pancras Old Church to an underground mausoleum in the town. The property is now known as Shelley Manor. When Lady Jane Shelley was to be buried in the family vault, it was discovered that in her copy of Adonaïs was an envelope containing ashes, which she had identified as belonging to her father-in-law.[36] The family had preserved the story that when Shelley's body had been burned, his friend Edward Trelawny had snatched the whole heart from the pyre.[35][37][38] These same accounts claim that the heart had been buried with Shelley's son, Percy. All accounts agree, however, that the remains now lie in the vault in the churchyard of St Peter's Church, Bournemouth.

For several years in the 20th century some of Trelawny's collection of Shelley ephemera, including a painting of Shelley as a child, a jacket, and a lock of his hair, were on display in "The Shelley Rooms", a small museum at Shelley Manor. When the museum finally closed in 2001, these items were returned to Lord Abinger, who descends from a niece of Lady Jane Shelley.[39]

Family history

Ancestry

Henry Shelley became father to younger Henry Shelley. This younger Henry had at least three sons. The youngest of them, Richard Shelley, was later married to Joan Fuste, daughter of John Fuste from Itchingfield, near Horsham, West Sussex.[citation needed] Their grandson John Shelley of Fen Place, Turners Hill, West Sussex, was married himself to Helen Bysshe, daughter of Roger Bysshe. Their son Timothy Shelley of Fen Place (born c.

1700) married widow Johanna Plum from New York City. Timothy and Johanna were the great-grandparents of Percy.

Family

Percy was born to Sir Timothy Shelley (7 September 1753 – 24 April 1844) and his wife Elizabeth Pilfold following their marriage in October 1791. His father was son and heir to Sir Bysshe Shelley, 1st Baronet of Castle Goring (21 June 1731 – 6 January 1815) by his wife Mary Catherine Michell (d. 7 November 1760). His mother was daughter of Charles Pilfold of Effingham. Through his paternal grandmother, Percy was a great-grandson to Reverend Theobald Michell of Horsham. Through his maternal lineage, he was a cousin of Thomas Medwin — a childhood friend and Shelley's biographer.[40]

Percy was the eldest of six children. His younger siblings were:
John Shelley of Avington House (15 March 1806 – 11 November 1866; married on 24 March 1827 Elizabeth Bowen (d. 28 November 1889));
Mary Shelley (NB. not to be confused with his wife);
Elizabeth Shelley (d. 1831);
Hellen Shelley (d. 10 May 1885);
Margaret Shelley (d. 9 July 1887).

Shelley's uncle, brother to his mother Elizabeth Pilfold, was Captain John Pilfold, a famous Naval Commander who served under Admiral Nelson during the Battle of Trafalgar.[41]

Descendants

Three children survived Shelley: Ianthe and Charles, his daughter and son by Harriet; and Percy Florence Shelley, his son by Mary. Charles, who suffered from tuberculosis, died in 1826 after being struck by lightning during a rainstorm. Percy Florence, who eventually inherited the baronetcy in 1844, died without children.

Several members of the Scarlett family were born at Percy Florence's seaside home "Boscombe Manor" in Bournemouth. They were descendants of Percy Florence's and Jane Gibson's adopted daughter, Bessie Florence Gibson. The 1891 census shows Lady Jane Shelley, Percy Florence Shelley's widow living at Boscombe Manor with several great nephews. Percy Florence Shelley died in 1889, and his widow, the former Jane St. John (born Gibson) died in 1899.

The only lineal descendants of the poet are therefore the children of Ianthe. Ianthe Eliza Shelley was married in 1837 to Edward Jeffries Esdaile of Cothelstone Manor. The marriage resulted in the birth of three daughters, Ianthe Harriet Shelley (1839-1849), Eliza Margaret (1841-1930), and Mary Emily Sydney (1848-1854), and three sons, Charles Edward (1842-1842), Charles Edward Jeffries (1845-1922), and William (1846-1915). Ianthe died in 1876, and her only descendants result from the marriage of Charles Edward Jeffries Esdaile and Marion Maxwell Sandbach.[42]

Idealism

Shelley's unconventional life and uncompromising idealism, combined with his strong disapproving voice, made him an authoritative and much-denigrated figure during his life and afterward. He became an idol of the next two or three or even four generations of poets, including the important Victorian and Pre-Raphaelite poets Robert Browning, Alfred, Lord Tennyson, Dante Gabriel Rossetti, Algernon Charles Swinburne, as well as Lord Byron, Henry David Thoreau, W. B. Yeats, Aleister Crowley and Edna St. Vincent Millay, and poets in other languages such as Jan Kasprowicz, Rabindranath Tagore, Jibanananda Das and Subramanya Bharathy.

Nonviolence

Henry David Thoreau's civil disobedience and Mahatma Gandhi's passive resistance were influenced and inspired by Shelley's nonviolence in protest and political action.[43] It is known that Gandhi would often quote Shelley's Masque of Anarchy,[44] which has been called "perhaps the first modern it of the principle of nonviolent resistance."[45]

vegetarianism

Shelley wrote several essays on the subject of vegetarianism, the most prominent of which were "A Vindication of Natural Diet" (1813) and "On the Vegetable System of Diet".[46][47]

Shelley, in heartfelt dedication to sentient beings, wrote:[48] "If the use of animal food be, in consequence, subversive to the peace of human society, how unwarrantable is the injustice and the barbarity which is exercised toward these miserable victims. They are called into existence by human artifice that they may drag out a short and miserable existence of slavery and disease, that their bodies may be mutilated, their social feelings outraged. It were much better that a sentient being should never have existed, than that it should have existed only to endure unmitigated misery"; "Never again may blood of bird or beast/ Stain with its venomous stream a human feast,/ To the pure skies in accusation steaming"; and "It is only by softening and disguising dead flesh by culinary preparation that it is rendered susceptible of mastication or digestion, and that the sight of its bloody juices and raw horror does not excite intolerable loathing and disgust."[48] In Queen Mab: A Philosophical Poem (1813) he wrote about the change to a vegetarian diet: "And man ... no longer now/ He slays the lamb that looks him in the face,/ And horribly devours his mangled flesh."[49]

Social Justice

Shelley was a strong advocate for social justice for the "lower classes". He witnessed many of the same mistreatments occurring in the domestication and slaughtering of animals, and he became a fighter for the rights of all living creatures that he saw being treated unjustly.[48]

Legacy

Shelley's mainstream following did not develop until a generation after his death, unlike Lord Byron, who was popular among all classes during his lifetime despite his radical views. For decades after his death, Shelley was mainly appreciated by only the major Victorian poets, the pre-Raphaelites, the socialists and the labour movement. One reason for this was the extreme discomfort with Shelley's political radicalism which led popular anthologists to confine Shelley's reputation to the relatively sanitised "magazine" pieces such as "Ozymandias" or "Lines to an Indian Air".

He was admired by C. S. Lewis,[50] Karl Marx, Robert Browning, Henry Stephens Salt, Gregory Corso, George Bernard Shaw, Bertrand Russell, Isadora Duncan,[3] Constance Naden,[51] Upton Sinclair,[52] Gabriele d'Annunzio, Aleister Crowley and W. B. Yeats.[53] Samuel Barber, Sergei Rachmaninoff, Roger Quilter, Howard Skempton, John Vanderslice and Ralph Vaughan Williams composed music based on his poems.

Critics such as Matthew Arnold endeavoured to rewrite Shelley's legacy to make him seem a lyricist and a dilettante who had no serious intellectual position and whose longer poems were not worth study. Matthew Arnold famously described Shelley as a "beautiful and ineffectual angel". This position contrasted strongly with the judgement of the previous generation who knew Shelley as a sceptic and radical.

Many of Shelley's works remained unpublished or little known after his death, with longer pieces such as A Philosophical View of Reform existing only in manuscript till the 1920s. This contributed to the Victorian idea of him as a minor lyricist. With the inception of formal literary studies in the early twentieth century and the slow rediscovery and re-evaluation of his oeuvre by scholars such as Kenneth Neill Cameron, Donald H. Reiman and Harold Bloom, the modern idea of Shelley could not be more different.

Paul Foot, in his Red Shelley, has documented the pivotal role Shelley's works – especially Queen Mab — have played in the genesis of British radicalism. Although Shelley's works were banned from respectable Victorian households, litical writings were pirated by men such as Richard Carlile who rly went to jail for printing "seditious and blasphemous libel" (i.e. material proscribed by the government), and these cheap pirate editions reached hundreds of activists and workers throughout the nineteenth century.[54]

In other countries such as India, Shelley's works both in the original and in translation have influenced poets such as Rabindranath Tagore[55] and Jibanananda Das. A pirated copy of Prometheus Unbound dated 1835 is said to have been seized in that year by customs at Bombay.

Paul Johnson, in his book Intellectuals,[56] describes Shelley in a chapter titled "Shelley or the Heartlessness of Ideas ". In the book Johnson describes Shelley as an amoral person, who by borrowing money which he did not intend to return, and by seducing young innocent women who fell for him, destroyed the lives of everybody with whom he had interacted, including his own.

In 2005 the University of Delaware Press published an extensive two-volume biography by James Bieri. In 2008 the Johns Hopkins University Press published Bieri's 856-page one-volume biography, Percy Bysshe Shelley: A Biography.

The rediscovery in mid-2006 of Shelley's long-lost Poetical Essay on the Existing State of Things, as noted above, was slow to be followed up until the only known surviving copy was acquired by the Bodleian Library in Oxford as its 12 millionth book in November 2015 and made available online.[57] An analysis of the poem by the only person known to have examined the whole work at the time of the original discovery appeared in the Times Literary Supplement: H. R. Woudhuysen, "Shelley's Fantastic Prank", 12 July 2006.[58]

In 2007, John Lauritsen published The Man Who Wrote Frankenstein, in which he argued that Percy Bysshe Shelley's contributions to the novel were much more extensive than had previously been assumed.[59] It has been known and not disputed that Shelley wrote the Preface – although uncredited – and that he contributed at least 4,000–5,000 words to the novel. Lauritsen sought to show that Shelley was the primary author of the novel.

In 2008, Percy Bysshe Shelley was credited as the co-author of Frankenstein by Charles E. Robinson in a new edition of the novel entitled The Original Frankenstein published by the Bodleian Library in Oxford and by Random House in the US.[60] Robinson determined that Percy Bysshe Shelley was the co-author of the novel: "He made very significant changes in words, themes and style. The book should now be credited as 'by Mary Shelley with Percy Shelley'."[61]

In late 2014, Shelley's work led lecturers from the University of Pennsylvania[62] and New York University[63] to produce a MOOC on the life of Percy Shelley and Prometheus Unbound.[64][65]

In popular culture

Shelley is believed to have been the model for Marmion Herbert, one of two male protagonists in Benjamin Disraeli's 1837 novel Venetia; the other, Lord Cadurcis, being based on Lord Byron.[66]
Henry James's 1888 novella, The Aspern Papers relates a struggle to obtain some letters by Shelley years after his death. It was made into a stage play and an opera.
Spoon River Anthology by Edgar Lee Masters (1915) includes a poem Percy Bysshe Shelley[67] as the namesake of the speaker, whose ashes "were scattered near the pyramid of Caius Cestius / Somewhere near Rome."
Shelley is a character in T. Zachary Cotler's novel Ghost at the Loom (2014).
Howard Brenton's play, Bloody Poetry (1984), explores the complex relationships and rivalries between Shelley, Mary Shelley, Claire Clairmont and Byron.
Shelley's cremation at Viareggio and the removal of his heart by Trelawny are described in Tennessee Williams's 1953 play Camino Real by a fictional Lord Byron.

A visit to Lord Byron's estate by Shelley and Mary Shelley is the setting for Ken Russell's 1986 film Gothic.

The film Haunted Summer has a similar theme to Gothic and is also set in 1816.

Shelley's poems The Revolt of Islam and Indian Serenade are recited in Sally Potter's film Orlando

A fictional Shelley befriends cavalry officer Matthew Hervey in the 2002 Allan Mallinson novel A Call to Arms.

Novelist Julian Rathbone fictionalises Shelley in A Very English Agent (2002), wherein a 19th-century government spy tampers with the poet's boat, causing his death.

Shelley appears as himself in Peter Ackroyd's novel The Casebook of Victor Frankenstein (2008).

Shelley was played by Ben Lamb in Shared Experience's 2012 production, "Mary Shelley" by Helen Edmundson, at the Tricycle Theatre, London.[68][69]

Shelley's poem "Love's Philosophy" appears frequently in the second season of the mystery television series Twin Peaks.

Shelley's poem "Ozymandias" lends its name to an episode of Breaking Bad. AMC had a teaser trailer for the final season of the show in which Bryan Cranston reads the poem.

Shelley's work, particularly the poem "Love's Philosophy," is referenced in the Series 2 episode of Lewis (TV series) entitled "And the Moonbeams Kiss the Sea."

Shelley is portrayed in Blackadder's third season episode Ink and Incapability as one of Samuel Johnson admirers. He is played by Lee Cornes

Major works

(1810) Zastrozzi
(1810) Original Poetry by Victor and Cazire
(1810) Posthumous Fragments of Margaret Nicholson: Being Poems Found Amongst the Papers of That Noted Female Who Attempted the Life of the King in 1786
(1810 dated 1811) St. Irvyne; or, The Rosicrucian

(1811) Poetical Essay on the Existing State of Things

(1811) The Necessity of Atheism

(1812) The Devil's Walk: A Ballad

(1813) Queen Mab: A Philosophical Poem

(1814) A Refutation of Deism: In a Dialogue

(1815) Alastor, or The Spirit of Solitude

(1815) Wolfstein; or, The Mysterious Bandit (chapbook)

(1816) The Daemon of the World

(1816) Mont Blanc

(1817) Hymn to Intellectual Beauty (text)

(1817) Laon and Cythna; or, The Revolution of the Golden City: A Vision of the Nineteenth Century

(1817) The Revolt of Islam, A Poem, in Twelve Cantos

(1817) History of a Six Weeks' Tour through a part of France, Switzerland, Germany, and Holland (with Mary Shelley)

(1818) Ozymandias (text)

(1818) The Banquet (or The Symposium) by Plato, translation from Greek into English[70]

(1818) Rosalind and Helen: A Modern Eclogue

(1818) Lines Written Among the Euganean Hills, October 1818

(1819) The Cenci, A Tragedy, in Five Acts

(1819) Ode to the West Wind (text)

(1819) The Masque of Anarchy

(1819) Men of England

(1819) England in 1819

(1819) A Philosophical View of Reform (published in 1920)

(1819) Julian and Maddalo: A Conversation

(1820) Peter Bell the Third (published in 1839)

(1820) Prometheus Unbound, A Lyrical Drama, in Four Acts

(1820) To a Skylark

(1820) The Cloud

(1820) Oedipus Tyrannus; Or, Swellfoot The Tyrant: A Tragedy in Two Acts

(1820) The Witch of Atlas (published in 1824)

(1821) Adonaïs

(1821) Ion by Plato, translation from Greek into English
(1821) A Defence of Poetry (first published in 1840)
(1821) Epipsychidion
(1822) Hellas, A Lyrical Drama
(1822) The Triumph of Life (unfinished, published in 1824)

Short prose works[edit]
"The Assassins, A Fragment of a Romance" (1814)
"The Coliseum, A Fragment" (1817)
"The Elysian Fields: A Lucianic Fragment"
"Una Favola (A Fable)" (1819, originally in Italian)

Essays

The Necessity of Atheism (1811)
Declaration of Rights (1812)
A Letter to Lord Ellenborough (1812)
A Defence of Poetry
A Vindication of Natural Diet (1813)
On the Vegetable System of Diet (1814–1815; published 1929)
On Love (1818)
On Life (1819)
On a Future State (1815)
On The Punishment of Death
Speculations on Metaphysics (1814)
Speculations on Morals (1817)
On Christianity (incomplete, probably 1817; published 1859)
On the Literature, the Arts and the Manners of the Athenians
On The Symposium, or Preface to The Banquet Of Plato
On Friendship
On Frankenstein

Collaborations with Mary Shelley
(1817) History of a Six Weeks' Tour

(1818) Frankenstein; or, The Modern Prometheus[71][72]

(1820) Proserpine

(1820) Midas

Printed in Great Britain
by Amazon

83021451R00031

Dedication
This book is dedicated to
Kirsty, Janet's daughter
and
Janice, Andrew's partner

Contents

CONTENTS

Part One

Encountering God
in the Development of Sacraments

Reflection

Janet Sutton writes:

When I was first ordained I knew everything I needed to know about the sacraments—or rather, I thought I did. I "knew" there were two—baptism and Holy Communion. Both were a source of unrest within my first congregation: Holy Communion, because there was no agreement about whether or not children should be allowed to participate fully; and baptism, because there was a feeling that lots of families "used" the church to bring their babies for christening, never to be seen again.

In response to my congregation's discomfort I arranged short sessions after services for children (and any adults) who wanted to understand what Holy Communion was all about (there were always more adults than children); and set conditions for parents bringing their child for baptism. But as issues they came way down my list of priorities. Sacraments, I thought: I could take them or leave them.

Imagine my surprise when, on appointment to a role as a pioneer minister, I discovered that not *having Holy Communion was a source of distress to me. The truth was, I hadn't known a good thing until I lost it. Through celebrating the Eucharist among my own flock I had experienced a profound sense of God's unconditional love for me, a confirmation of my call to the ministry of word and sacrament, a strong bonding with the people gathered around me, and a sense of call and commission to take the love of Christ out into the world around me. Without it I felt a sense of deep loss, which remained until, two years later, my infant emerging church community shared bread and wine around a table.*

I was even more surprised, when I gave birth to my daughter, that my attitude to baptism was fundamentally challenged. I looked down at the tiny bundle in my arms with an immense sense of overwhelming responsibility, and wanted to do everything I could to bring her up well. That included having her "Christened." I had assumed that she would have a thanksgiving and naming ceremony.

"What's the difference between naming and baptism?" my then husband asked.

I explained about God being present in a special way during the sacramental act.

"Why wouldn't you want that?" he asked.

It did make logical sense, so I agreed. According to tradition I should have chosen godparents who would help me nurture my daughter in the faith. In reality I considered who I would trust to look after her if anything happened to her parents. My strong sacramental principles, founded on a solid understanding of the Reformed tradition, failed me. Because this was real life—my life. And that's not the same as sitting in an ivory tower deciding which theologians were correct in their centuries-old wisdom. And so I began to encounter some of the dissonance experienced by the majority of the normal, vaguely God-believing members of the British population. Because what the church says, and what real life and experience teach us, are not necessarily the same thing . . .

1

Sacraments in a Time of . . .

This book has been written and published during a time of radical change, not just for Christianity, but for the entire world. The demise of the Christendom epoch and critical decline of the institutional church are mirrored in every aspect of life, from the complete loss of confidence in inherited Western political systems to impending ecological disaster and the possible destruction of the planet.

Added to this, in the final weeks of preparing this work for publication, we have experienced the onset of the COVID-19 pandemic and its consequences. Set against this background, academic debates about how many sacraments there are and who should be allowed to preside at them might seem rather irrelevant.

And yet, this has been a time of profound ecclesiological unsettling within many Christian traditions, particularly when it comes to the celebration of the sacraments. For some, whose sacramental theology requires the physical presence of a gathered believing community to make them efficacious, celebrating sacraments or ordinances, either alone or digitally "on screen," is not possible. Nor has it been possible, for very different reasons, for those whose ecclesiology demands the presence and presidency of an ordained priest together with consecrated elements.

Any book about the sacraments is, first, a book about *identity*. It is through the celebration of rituals and ordinances within a particular context (which might or might not be described as sacramental) that individual and corporate Christian identity is created. In other words, how we define ourselves as believers in Jesus and what we seek in terms of Christian community are shaped, broadly, by how we experience Christ in our midst through a set of practices.

Sacraments are part of those practices of the Christian community, just as prayer is another. The majority of members of the Protestant tradition acknowledge only baptism and Eucharist (or Holy Communion) as sacraments, whereas in the Western Catholic tradition there are a further five: anointing of the sick, confirmation, holy orders, marriage, and penance/reconciliation (we explain these more fully later). Some Christian movements do not have sacraments and others prefer the term *ordinance* for such practices. These often depend on theological traditions and historical contexts.

Second, this is a book about *context*. It is important that Christians, congregations, and theologians re-engage in discussion about the role of the sacraments in the new and developing post-Christendom context.

> Christendom is the concept of western civilization as having a religious arm (the church) and a secular arm (civil government), both of which are united in their adherence to the Christian faith, which is seen as the so-called soul of Europe or the West. The essence of the idea is the assertion that western civilization is Christian. Within this Christian civilization, the church and the state have different roles to play, but, since membership in both is coterminous, both can be seen as aspects of one unified reality—Christendom.[1]

Post-Christendom or, more popularly, "after Christendom," is what is happening now in Britain, Europe, and metropolitan Australia, and its seeds are now beginning to be seen in North America.

Christianity comes in more forms than could possibly be calculated, the identity of each tradition being shaped by its historical and current context. In addition, how each tradition's key thinkers and leaders have encouraged the way the Bible should be read and interpreted over years, decades, or centuries, will influence both belief and praxis.

Divisions have been created, wars fought, and even new societies founded over what might today be considered small issues of theology. However, to believe these are small is to underestimate the extent to which sacraments, throughout church history, have been both instrumental in and integral to the life of the church—and to its authority within society. Whether or not Christians from different traditions can share in the Eucharist together remains one of the most divisive issues in the church; indeed one of the purposes of this

---

1. Carter, *Re-thinking Christ*, 14.

book is to enable such difficult theological issues to be considered in a different light.

As this book was being completed, social media came alive with debates among clergy about their responses to COVID-19, questioning whether the Eucharist can faithfully be celebrated "virtually" during times of social distancing and physical lockdown. Predominantly for pastoral reasons, those in leadership have relaxed their various stances, providing guidance they consider will be helpful for members and adherents during such exceptional circumstances. For some, these emergency measures have proved decidedly unhelpful: the seeming abandonment of the rich principles of their own tradition, which they consider an integral part of their identity as a follower of Christ.

At this point in time (Easter, 2020) it can be only an assumption on our part that we are living through a pivotal moment, not just for the church, but for the whole world. The impact of COVID-19 on social, political, and economic systems, as well as faith traditions of all kinds across the world, cannot even begin to be estimated. On first drafting this book, our initial premise was that the church, an institution which has nurtured and served us throughout two millennia, is no longer fit for purpose. The current pandemic has exposed some of this even more starkly; but at the same time perhaps it has been the jolt the churches across different traditions needed to make them assess their success (or otherwise) in terms of mission and ministry within their communities, and to give them license to review the efficacy (or otherwise) of their ecclesial and sacramental theologies and practices. In short, how can the church continue to facilitate human-divine[2] encounter, such that Jesus-shaped communities can experience for themselves the transcendent but very real presence of a God who stands among them in the person of Christ?

This brings us to the third major theme to be explored in this book: *tradition*. On the surface this appears to be an ecclesiological theme—the way church in all its different forms organizes itself. However, there is a far deeper issue at play here: it is how Christians, now and through the ages, perceive God to be at work in the world through the power of the Holy Spirit. It is a subject that takes us to the heart of the Christian faith as well as to a single day in history almost two thousand years ago.

Belief in the power of the Holy Spirit, God's agent in the world, unites Christians across the globe; yet the form taken, the manifestation, and even

---

2. We recognize that people encounter God in many circumstances, which find written testimony in the Christian Bible and their living echo in the sacraments. We continually use "human-divine" to refer to such encounters, and offer further theological reasoning for this choice in chapter 14.

the words used to describe the Holy Spirit—it/her/him—can be causes of major division. As we will discover in this book, belief in how the Holy Spirit is at work in the world is intimately connected with attitudes towards ritual practices, whether they be described as "sacramental" or not.

Ultimately, this is a book about human-divine encounter and the resultant understandings of how Christians relate to and with a *covenant* God, whether it be through signs, symbols, words, or actions. This book exists to explore the way God breaks into the lives of individuals and Christian communities, and how that in-breaking is both mediated and experienced through the rituals, ordinances, or other practices considered sacramental within each particular Christian community's tradition.

One of the keys to unlocking the nature of the church during Christendom, and therefore moving towards understanding it after Christendom, is to examine how it has developed and been understood through the sacraments. In what we would term "the shift into post-Christendom," the definitions of what constitutes "church" and what it means to be a follower of Jesus within an ecclesial community are open to discussion. The church of today is emerging in many places as a new entity—or collection of different entities—with Jesus Christ in common. In many emerging communities there are no longer set ideas about where and in what form Christians meet, how they worship, how they explore and understand the Bible, and how they experience Christ in their midst through sacramental practice.

It will be for future ecclesiastical historians to determine how much of a pivotal transition the church now finds itself within. And in such a state of flux, we do not claim that this volume could, or does, give the last word upon sacraments after Christendom. Rather, we intend to provide a contribution to the debate about how, what, where, when, and why sacramental theology and practice might be shaped for the future. To ignore engaging in such conversations risks losing some of the God-given vitality that we will need in reaching out to meet the missionary challenges of our post-Christendom age.

The Nature of Sacraments

Thomas Cranmer, in the preface to the Anglican Book of Common Prayer (1549), described the sacraments as "an outward and visible sign of an inward and invisible means of grace." He was using a formulation dating back as far as the North African theologian and philosopher, Augustine of Hippo (354–430), one also used by Anselm (ca. 1033–1109) and Aquinas (1225–1274).

This helpful description has survived through the modern era and remains useful contemporarily in the nurture of new Christians.[3]

What such a definition clearly implies is that a sacramental moment involving reciprocal activity between God and humanity is an "in-breaking of God's holiness" into a particular earthly "moment." This phrasing of the "in-breaking of God's holiness" comes directly from the globally seminal work of the German philosopher and theologian, Rudolf Otto (1869–1937)—*The Idea of the Holy*. Although it is impossible to translate Otto's thesis in its fullest meaning into English, Otto uses the term "holiness" to describe the nature and activity of God. Using the term "numinous" from the Latin *numen* (meaning "holy"), Otto sought to demonstrate that "the holy" has a divine power, both mysterious and fascinating.

One of the other key parts of Otto's thesis—"*Gottes ist ganz andere*" (Ger.)—is often rendered as "God is wholly other." In both the sacraments and other sacramental moments, it is (at least in part) the encounter with that holiness—that wholly other nature of God—which makes it transformative for the individual person. In romantic terms, one could describe this as "where heaven and earth meet."

In his 2020 book, *Recapturing an Enchanted World: Ritual and Sacrament in the Free Churches*, John D. Rempel explores how, through rituals, customs, feasts, and festivals, communities of faith have incorporated a "sacramentality of time" into their daily lives. He notes that, in Judaic, then early Christian, thought, "time had a forward movement toward the fullness of God's reign at the end of time and through eternity."[4] By adopting the Sabbath, observing the Passover, and celebrating the resurrection on Easter Day, participants were entering into a *kairos*, or sacramental, moment, "one in which God's Kingdom becomes tangible."[5]

This experience of history-changing human-divine encounter can be found time and again in the Bible, as mere humans come face to face with the holiness, glory, and power of God.

- When Moses encounters God in the burning bush, he is reminded by the voice within that he is standing on holy ground and is to acknowledge this by taking off his sandals (Exod 3:1–14).

---

3. Formal teaching within such nurture is sometimes called "the catechism" and those being nurtured "the catechumenate."

4. Rempel, *Recapturing*, 55–60.

5. Rempel, *Recapturing*, 55–60.

- When Isaiah the prophet enters the temple and sees "the glory of the Lord" filling the space while six-winged angels attend the moment and bring a burning coal to salve the prophet's unclean lips (Isa 6:1–6).

- When Peter, James, and John are with Jesus on the mountain, encountering Moses and Elijah, it becomes a transfiguring moment (Matt 17:1–13).

- When Peter encounters Jesus for a Galilean beach breakfast barbecue after the resurrection, he is empowered afresh to recognize Jesus' call to holiness in his own life (John 21:15–19).

However, despite fitting Rempel's definition of "sacramental moments," none of these events have ever been deemed to be "sacraments." As writers, we recognize that the in-breaking of "the holy" into the life of God's people cannot be limited to just a certain number of practices or actions. As we later explain, while the assumption is that there are a finite number of in-breaking communal practices which can be declared as sacraments, we believe that sacramental activity is broader than that.

It is therefore useful to make clear at the outset our view that an event or practice can be "sacramental" without being labelled as "a sacrament." We view sacraments as corporate activities of a Jesus-believing community, through which we are re-membered as part of the corporate people of God, past, present, and future. That re-membering is a particular moment of grace, which incorporates us afresh within the body of Christ, as we recognize Christ's presence in our midst. In that "moment of grace," God acts transformatively in our lives through the power of the Holy Spirit. Such "moments of grace" can occur in another time, place, or activity.

Just How Accessible Is This?

When speaking to those outside the church, not just to those who have consciously rejected inherited models of church, but also those who have never encountered Christianity or Christian community, we realize that we may as well speak gobbledygook as use formal definitions of sacraments. How are those without even a basic knowledge of Christian tradition and theology supposed to understand the spiritual difference between the visible and invisible, or the theological "means of grace," or implications and practical outworkings of it? Is *grace* even a word that people would generally use?

Our thesis is that sacramental praxis plays a vital role in shaping Christian identity, both individually and corporately. The nature of shared experience within Christian communities is vital to understanding how those Christians perceive the role and place of sacraments within their communities.

We suggest that the human believing community is an essential parallel expression of the divine community. This has been expressed by many writers but particularly eloquently by Leonardo Boff:

> This mystery [the Trinity] becomes embodied in history, because it is organised in groups and communities. Communities in turn assume the elements of each age, so that the church has as many faces as the incarnations it has undergone throughout history . . . The Blessed Trinity is a sacramental mystery. In other words, it is something that appears in many signs, that can always be known; yet our effort to know never ends.[6]

As the church navigates post-Christendom, these new incarnations become key to reaching those with no background knowledge of the Christian faith or experience of church culture. Many British primary school children have little or no knowledge, and certainly not significant understandings, of the Jesus narrative—except perhaps a garbled version of the infancy narratives which they gained from "nativity plays." There is a well-known scene in the film *Love Actually*, where one character has been given the role of "first lobster" in her school nativity play. "There was more than one lobster at the birth of Jesus?" responds the child's mother, incredulous. "Duh!" says the child, as though not thinking there would be a lobster present was a ridiculous thought![7]

While there are those for whom the sacraments are both transformative and life-affirming, for many people the term *sacrament* has no meaning at all. Therefore, in everyday terms, we often find ourselves explaining the sacraments as a particular means (or activity) of approaching God and molding individual and corporate Christian identity. Given the fact that only 6 percent of the English population regularly attend Christian worship, this lack of understanding of something as central to Christianity as sacraments demonstrates another reason why this book needs to engage with the subject.[8]

How We Use Scripture and Sources

Both of us have engaged with biblical studies at postgraduate level and have practical knowledge of how Scripture is generally used by the Christian

---

6. Boff, *Holy Trinity*, 108, 115.

7. https://www.youtube.com/watch?v=9chdp8izEtk.

8. https://faithsurvey.co.uk/download/gb-church-attendance-1980-2015.pdf.

tradition. We will refer to texts in what is traditionally referred to as the "Old Testament" as the Hebrew Scriptures, and to "New Testament" texts more often as the type of text they are (Gospel, epistle, etc.) or more generally as the "apostolic writings." What we are seeking to avoid is the Christendom trap of creating an implied superiority for the New Testament over the older Hebrew Scriptures.

We have to rely on Christian tradition and list biblical references in ways accessible to the reader and as advocated by our publisher. References to the Christian Bible are normally given by three pieces of information: the name of the book involved; the chapter; then the verse or verses, e.g., Ruth 3:9 or John 10:10. This will be the style adopted throughout our text. Unless stated otherwise, the translation used is the New Revised Standard Version.

It may seem obvious but in any exploration of Christian theology, "church practices," or personal discipleship, one rapidly encounters statements such as "the Bible says . . ." or "Jesus teaches that . . ." What does this mean? Few readers will refer to the Hebrew Scriptures, or the Gospels or apostolic writings in their original Greek, and thus must recognize that they are using an English translation or paraphrase, which may have come via a previous Latin translation. We will have to return to looking at the nuance of particular words or biblical phrases and their implications for this book.

Even the simple "Jesus says . . ." needs reviewing. The church is indebted to the German theologian Joachim Jeremias (1900–1979) for enabling believers to understand clearly the difference between the "actual words" (*ipsissima verba*) and the "actual voice" (*ipsissima vox*) of Jesus. Did Jesus actually say the words attributed to him on the pages of the most reputable biblical translation? Let us explain with two examples:

- Semitic languages, such as the Aramaic that Jesus spoke, are very pictorial and do not use verbs. Jesus would almost certainly not have been speaking Greek when he reportedly said, "This is my body, broken for you" at the Last Supper (Luke 22:19) but Aramaic, saying "This, my body, for you." How many centuries of argument about the Mass/Eucharist/Holy Communion have been built on the Greek which Jesus is supposed to have said?

- Equally, Matthew records Jesus saying, at the end of his earthly ministry, "Go into all the world, preach the good news, baptize them in the name of the Father, Son, and Holy Spirit . . ." (Matt 28:18–19, our translation) several weeks before Pentecost (when the Spirit came upon the believers) and decades before anyone had a clear trinitarian understanding. So have we got the actual words (*verba*) or just the voice (*vox*) of Jesus here?

How important is this for understanding the sacramental development of baptism?

As writers, we have great love and respect for how the Bible *can* teach us when our theology and practice is determined by it, but we have to have integrity and recognize the differences between Jesus' "actual words" and Jesus' "actual voice" in following his call.[9]

We have both been influenced by the Wisdom tradition of biblical scholarship, which uses the person of "wisdom" (Gk.: *Sophia*) to "explain" the character of the divine breath or Holy Spirit (Prov 8:1).[10] To maintain a sense of linguistic balance, we have adopted masculine pronouns when writing about Jesus and chosen to use feminine pronouns for the Holy Spirit.

Much recent theological thought has been stimulated by current trends in biblical scholarship associated with how the earliest disciples and Jesus-shaped communities both met and worshiped. The power of the works of Robert Banks, Andrew McGowan, and Hal Taussig among others is that they utilize not just the biblical text, but also other sources, including archaeological, literary, and historical ones. Their work draws attention to the counter-cultural nature not just of liturgy, but also of the placing of members of the earliest Christian communities (slave and free sharing the common cup, or women and slaves being given equal placings to men, etc.). Their books or journal articles have been influential in locating much early Christian meeting/ worship within the context of a Greco-Roman banquet, as well as exploring use of liturgy within the context of earliest Christian worship.[11]

Similarly we are encouraged by the much-respected (but little known beyond Anglican circles) liturgist and theologian, A. H. Couratin, whose legacy has creatively influenced so much current UK denominational and ecumenical theological education. Couratin and others acknowledged the vitality of the pre-Christendom church, which grew through the work of particular influential figures and a rich variety of specific Christian communities rather than definitive liturgies. Couratin maintains this allowed no real liturgical history pre-Christendom but does offer an embryonic prehistory. This widely accepted argument affects how writers, academics, and readers treat and use original sources. A primary document is the New Testament's apostolic writings whereas rites from a particularly geographic church can act only as indicators of the ways in which Christian thought was developing.

9. Jeremias, *Eucharistic Words*; Jeremias, *New Testament Theology*.

10. Daise and Charlesworth, eds., *Light in a Spotless Mirror*.

11. Banks, *Going to Church*; McGowan, *Ancient Christian Worship*; Smith and Taussig, *Many Tables*.

One of our influences is ourselves. We are both white, well educated, middle class, and financially supported (salaried or pensioned) by different denominations as ordained United Reformed Church ministers. We live in the UK and work among congregations struggling with the issues associated with the declining Christendom church. While we can try to understand "world church" perspectives, in reality we can write only from our own, and we recognize those limitations.

Semper Reformanda

As we both hail from different parts of the Reformed tradition, we are accustomed to the rallying cry: *"Semper reformanda"*—"always reforming." In his *Perpetually Reforming* volume, John Bradbury reminds us that our identity in and through Jesus Christ is found in how the church continually and repeatedly shares the nature of God in the outworking of its life in the world.[12]

In one sense, any Christian from the Reformed tradition must be prepared to countenance significant change in the way that Jesus-shaped discipleship is undertaken, both individually and corporately. It is no accident that, in its "Statement of Nature, Faith and Order," the UK's United Reformed Church not only allows, but positively encourages, us to change both how we articulate and practice our discipleship and our collective trajectory in following the leading of the Holy Spirit and the prayerful discernment of the denomination's people.[13] We are thankful to be ministers within such a forward- and God-ward-looking company, within the broader contemporary "Jesus movement."

We realize that how Christian communities agree to travel and learn together becomes an informal covenant, enabling God's in-breaking, helping to forge a shared identity in Christ. In sharing this earthly pilgrimage, we uncover our missional purpose and rework the forms and expressions of our faith, because of our church tradition or our cherished biblical values and interpretations.

So What Lies Ahead?

This book is divided into three parts:

- The first part lays trails, sows seeds, and sets some parameters for our discussion. Following this Introduction, there are four chapters, beginning

---

12. Bradbury, *Perpetually Reforming*, 78–79.

13. Thompson, ed., *Stating the Gospel*, 262–65.

with one examining how the "Jesus movement" came together corporately in sharing the dominical sacraments. The next chapter examines the issues around the development of sacraments within the Christendom church, while the third highlights several of those issues created by the innate challenges of the post-Christendom church. Finally in this part, we examine some of the theology and theory that we believe is necessary when exploring and calibrating the relative nature of sacraments. The images of covenant,, tradition, context, and identity, both in Christ and as members of Christian communities, will recur in the successive chapters of this book.

- The second and longest part of the book comprises two longer and a set of shorter chapters concerning particular aspects of life and faith that have been described as sacramental, and that some would call sacraments. The first of those chapters reexamines what baptism and Eucharist as sacraments, which nearly all Christians practice, have come to mean today. The second looks at those practices which the Catholic and most of the Orthodox traditions declare as sacraments. Then the four shorter chapters each examine the claims of another aspect of Christian life, which some regard as sacramental.

- The final part of this volume has three concluding chapters in which we outline what have, for us, become the central issues and questions which must form part of the discussion. We also offer some conclusions of our own. There is also a select bibliography.

We are believers in the encouragement of a "currency of ideas," which can enrich a dialogue or conversation about pivotal theological or philosophical moments and concepts. As we have already stated, rather than providing definitive solutions to issues surrounding sacramental theology and practice, the aim of this book is to enable readers to grapple themselves with what the sacraments and sacramentality mean to them.

2

The "Jesus Movement"
and the Dominical Sacraments

The earthly Jesus was known as "Jesus of Nazareth" and sometimes called *rabbi*, the Hebrew name for teacher. His was an orthodox Jewish upbringing, and the world he inhabited would have been one set within that context, with its annual cycle of feasts and festivals. As yet there was no "Christian church," and the feast we now know as Pentecost was, to Jesus, *Shavuot*, the "Feast of Weeks," a festival to commemorate God revealing to Moses the five books of the Torah and the harvesting of the wheat in the Holy Land.

"Turn around, for the Reign of God is upon You"

From the Gospel narratives it is clear that Jesus' followers were numerous, attracted by his ability to perform miracles and gathering to hear his teaching about the coming "reign of God." This is the exciting and recurring if not demanding and arresting call, which permeates the ministry of Jesus of Nazareth. The authors' version of Matthew 3:2 is a translation of the Greek. Often rendered: "Repent, for the kingdom of God is at hand," the verse could just as easily be written as: "Turn around, for the reign of God is overtaking you" or "is almost within grasp." The phrasing implies an overwhelming urgency, something just out of reach yet with a need for response, as well as something not previously experienced.

Central to his earthly public ministry is Jesus' own teaching and demonstrative lifestyle of the "reign of God." While theologians, preachers, and biblical translators have been content to use the phrase the "kingdom of God," its meaning is increasingly being lost. In classic Hebrew, therefore pre-Christian, thought, the Messiah would come to reign over earthly territory like some super-monarch. Jesus' manner, style, and teaching were entirely different, having little to do with territorial ownership and focusing on the transformation of hearts and minds. Liberation theologians took up this refreshing realignment of biblical thinking, consistently referring to the "reign of God," in preference to the "kingdom of God."[1] This found its practical outworking in the sacramental life and the nature of the base church communities, in Central and South America. In addition, postmodern feminist and linguistic commentators question the use of the word *kingdom*, due to its patriarchal association—preferring the equally accessible but more appropriate term *reign*.[2]

Identifying with the Jesus Movement

In their seminal work *The Shaping of Things to Come*, the writers Alan Hirsch and Michael Frost highlight the importance of understanding the world and person of Jesus when developing any sort of Christian theology, one centered around the words, works, and ways of Jesus, who became known as "the Christ." They argue for a "Messianic spirituality," which genuinely engages with a first-century Semitic worldview so different in nature from Western culture with its philosophical roots based in Platonic Hellenism. Far from being an "other-world" God, the divine Creator of first-century Judaism was deeply engaged with the universe of God's own making. That humankind was a mere reflection of the God who created them was understood in temporal, almost physical terms. This God is one who searches out the faithful, intervenes in human affairs, and engages in a revelatory process passed down through the generations and recorded for the benefit of those grasping for fuller relationship with the one they believe created them. This is a God whose reign is exercised through those in relationship with this God-who-became-personally-known in Jesus.

There is something both intimate and earthy about the way God takes on human form. The Gospel accounts make it clear that Jesus isn't afraid of getting stuck in: touching and being touched by others. He "lays hands" on all those who come to him at sundown, heals using a mixture of mud, spittle, and touch, and when a woman who has been suffering from menstrual problems for eighteen years touches his cloak, Jesus feels the power go out of him and

1. See Gutierrez, "Option for the Poor"; Sobrino, "Reign of God in Liberation Theology"; Magana, "Ecclesiology in the Theology of Liberation."

2. This is explained more fully in *Shalom*: "In today's world of politically correct thought and speech, Christian believers will find it much easier to speak of the reign of God." Francis, *Shalom*, 27–28.

declares her faith has made her well. He is renowned for dining with sinners and befriending the lost. But the most revealing encounters of all, those which flesh out Jesus' identity as the most unconventional of saviors, invariably include touch. He lays hands on and blesses children, is anointed by a woman who wipes away the perfume with her hair, washes the feet of the disciples and, after the final meal and walk in the garden, is betrayed by the most intimate of touches—a kiss.

God taking on bodily form in the person of Jesus signifies the beginning of the restoration of the relationship between God and humanity, which had been ruptured during "the fall" (Rom 5:10–14; 1 Cor 15:20–26). The God who walked in the garden of Eden, searching for the shamed Adam and Eve, is the same God who befriends, heals, serves, and commands those he encounters in the everyday ordinariness of first-century Palestine. This concept of bodily redemption is then modeled in the earliest Jesus-believing communities, who describe themselves as the "body of Christ" (1 Cor 12). Being Christ in the world was symbolic of the understanding that, through their corporate faith in Jesus, they had through the power of the Holy Spirit *become* part of the rich history of God's people, past, present, and future.

This corporate embodiment found its outworking, both through their tangible attachment to each other and how they reached out together to the world around them. The picture painted by Luke of the earliest disciples in Jerusalem is a powerful example of incarnational mission and ministry. Such a context provides inspiration for how the Christian life can and should be lived today:

> Awe came upon everyone, because many wonders and signs were being done by the apostles. All who believed were together and had all things in common; they would sell their possessions and goods and distribute the proceeds to all, as any had need. Day by day, as they spent much time together in the temple, they broke bread at home and ate their food with glad and generous hearts, praising God and having the goodwill of all the people. And day by day the Lord added to their number those who were being saved. (Acts 2:42–47)

By the time Paul wrote to the infant churches, a common corporate identity and pattern of worship was emerging. The Jesus-believing communities met weekly over a meal, during which bread and wine was shared in remembrance of Christ.[3] Baptism, as the ceremony of initiation into the community

---

3. Taussig, *In the Beginning*, 40–49, 130–39.

of believers, was prepared for and undertaken, either as individuals or as a household. These activities became the symbols of the Jesus movement.

They worked out how to elect and authorize leaders (Acts 6:1–6), deal with questions of marriage (1 Cor 7), and prepare for the afterlife in the expectation that Christ was coming again soon (2 Cor 5:1–10). It seems that, as the emerging Jesus-believing communities worked out a way to live, love, and worship together, their commitment was not just to walking the way of Jesus together, but actually embodying it (Acts 2:42–47; 4:32–35). Although the Scriptures use no sacramental terminology, it is clear that a pattern was emerging organically that reflected the beliefs of the nascent communities and marked them out as individual members of Christ's body; this was tradition in the making.

This was the beginning of the Jesus movement, commonly known as "the way." It was at Antioch that these followers of Jesus were first called Christians (Acts 11:26)—by their opponents. Documented Roman history shows that Christians were an oppressed and persecuted group; it is not myth that some died in the arena as lion bait. Patterns of communal life and ministry varied regionally, although the principles stayed the same; there was a common *habitus*—"pattern of Jesus-shaped discipleship."[4] Christianity was truly countercultural to mainstream Roman norms, allowing slave and free, female and male to mix freely, displaying what the biblical scholar John Crossan calls "open commensality" (eating together) and "radical egalitarianism."[5] The Jesus movement, which declared in its communal life and talk the nature of the reign of God, continued to grow.

Activity of the Holy Spirit

While the humanity of Jesus' identity and teachings is without doubt a key factor in shaping the earliest Christian communities, the activity of the Holy Spirit was also a key influencer. While it was understood that *ruach*, God's Spirit, could and did abide within human beings (Ps 51:10–12, 17), the force with which the apostles receive the *pneuma* (Greek term for the Holy Spirit) on the day of Pentecost appears to be in a totally different league.[6] It gives them power to speak in tongues previously unknown to them, to perform miracles of healing, and, as Paul describes later, to "know the mind of Christ" (1 Cor 2:16).

4. Kreider, *Patient Ferment*, ch. 3.
5. Crossan, *Jesus*, 66.
6. Moule, *Holy Spirit*, 7–17.

The importance of the presence and activity of the Holy Spirit in the earliest Christian communities cannot be underestimated; indeed the Greek word *pneuma* is used more than 280 times in the New Testament. In the first chapter of Acts, Luke records Jesus, as he prepares to ascend into heaven, as instructing the apostles "through the Holy Spirit" and promising that they will "be baptized with the Holy Spirit not many days from now" (Acts 1:2, 5). The Spirit is a force that will empower them to "be my witnesses in Jerusalem, Judea and Samaria, and to the ends of the earth" (Acts 1:8), not a small feat for a group of eleven Galileans of assorted professions.

C. F. D. Moule, in his classic work *The Holy Spirit*, describes the "work of the Holy Spirit" as inspirer and life-giver, the source of the believers' new identity as members of God's family, whether they are of Jewish or non-Jewish heritage.[7] They "pray in the Spirit" (Eph 6:18; Jude 20), speak the truth in the power of the Spirit (Acts 5:3–9), and are baptized with the Spirit, as foretold by John the Baptist (Mark 1.8//).

The latter is not a description of the practice of baptism with water, which is described below. It is instead the power by which the believers understood themselves able to fulfill their role as members of the body of Christ day by day. Later we shall see how key the understanding of how the third person of the Trinity functions is to the development of the church and its sacramental theology and practice.

Baptism

Other than through the ministry of John the Baptist, baptism does not feature strongly in the canonical Gospels. We have no biblical record that Jesus called for or administered baptism to others; nor do we have any such record of "the disciples" who accompanied him administering baptism during Jesus' "earthly ministry."

It was (and remains) common Jewish practice to undergo ritual washing.[8] For this purpose, ritual baths called *mikveh* fed by streams of "living waters" (i.e., flowing) and also ritual washing using water kept in large jars were used. The narrative of the wedding at Cana in Galilee in John 2 refers to such large stone jars. So any movement or community of people who had contact with Judaism would immediately understand the practice of ritual washing.

It would have been nothing new when "John the Baptizer suddenly appeared in the desert, announcing the reign of God, calling for his hearers to

---

7. Moule, *Holy Spirit*, 27–30.
8. Berlin and Grossman, eds., "Cleanliness," 174.

repent and be baptized." This is a loose paraphrase of our translation of the Synoptic Gospels' description of the beginning of the ministry of John the Baptist. It would not be surprising for God-fearing Jews to find themselves both challenged and upset by the radical preaching of John the Baptist, who called for his hearers to repent and be baptized. Such faithful Jews who followed the traditions and demands of the law, including all those ritual lustrations, are challenged by John's diet and wild appearance, as well as the rooting of his challenge in Isaiah's prophetic call (Isa 61:1–3; cf. Luke and John).

However, what was different when Jesus came to be baptized in the river Jordan by John was how visibly the Holy Spirit descended upon Jesus. God's voice from heaven affirms his identity: "This is my beloved Son, in whom I am well pleased." Not only was this the empowerment and beginning of Jesus' itinerant, adult public ministry; it was also the introduction of a completely new understanding of what takes place during baptism. While previously the immersion and rising of the candidate symbolized repentance, forgiveness, and a fresh start, Christian baptism represented a change in their very identity. And the voice from heaven and accompanying dove signified the bestowal of the Holy Spirit, not only on Jesus, but also on every future person entering into Christian baptism.

Within decades, the post-resurrection, post-Pentecost Christian community practiced this form of baptism, as a mark of both discipleship and personal activist acceptance of the reign of God. Baptism and the reception of the Holy Spirit went hand in hand. Acts 2:41 records that in response to Peter's pentecostal preaching: "Many of his hearers believed his message and were baptized—about three thousand people were added to their number on that day" (our translation). Considering the experience of tongues of fire and thunderous sounds followed by superhuman abilities to speak and to heal, it is unsurprising that those witnessing what happened wanted to become recipients.

However there is clearly more to it than that. Something had happened to the apostles between Jesus' resurrection and ascension and the "day of Pentecost." Or have we an unsolvable mystery that Jesus' disciples had practiced some kind of baptism during his earthly ministry and that the Gospel writers thought it of such little importance that they did not mention it? Established biblical commentators (e.g., Bruce, Dunn, Marshall[9]) focus on the practicalities of conducting three thousand adult baptisms or whether Jerusalem had enough interested listeners or how long it would take to conduct this—rather than focusing on the substantive issue of baptism appearing as such normative practice so quickly. Or, as some have posited, is the mention of baptism in the

9. Bruce, *Book of Acts*; Dunn, *Acts of the Apostles*; Marshall, *Acts*.

Greek text of Acts 2:41 a later interpolation by theologians and/or translators seeking biblical justification for a growing, commonplace practice? Biblical scholarship recognizes that (in the use of different linguistic styles or implied references) at different points of the text there have been additions to the narrative; these are known as interpolations.

Certainly, baptism was commonplace enough that in Luke's record of Philip's encounter with the Ethiopian eunuch the latter could say: "Here is water! What is to prevent me from being baptized?" (Acts 8:38). Whether this is a literal description of the event or later biblical interpolation, certainly it indicates that "baptism" quickly arrived as the chosen way to declare one's allegiance to "the way" of Jesus. It is only later in Acts 11:26 that Luke's narrative records the Antioch declaration that such believers were then called Christians. This implies that the Ethiopian's baptism was either a major tradition-forming event, or at least made to appear one for the purposes of the early movement.

As previously stated, the post-resurrection, post-Pentecost Christian community practiced baptism as a mark of personal discipleship declaring allegiance to Jesus. The majority of biblical scholars agree that most of the Pauline and other so-called New Testament letters were written before the Gospels.[10] In several of those letters, Paul particularly deals with issues to do with Christian baptism, describing it as the way believers are incorporated into "the body of Christ," the church.[11] Within decades, baptism had clearly become a widespread practice of the Christian community: "Paul can write of baptism as a given, from which theological conclusions can be drawn (Romans 6:3–11)."[12]

Within a further century, baptismal practice within the major Christian communities had developed into an annual liturgical rite, following a lengthy catechumenate[13]—but more of this in the next chapter. In matters concerning the development of various rites, the Anglican scholar Couratin has argued persuasively that prior to the fourth century common liturgies did not really exist (except potentially in specific locations, such as Rome) but that biblical practices did.[14] Couratin was effectively a forerunner of the thinking that Cheslyn Jones, N. T. Wright, and more recently McGowan have developed; we can demonstrate that something was a biblical practice but did not necessarily

10. Dunn, *Unity and Diversity*, 152.

11. Cullmann, *Baptism in the New Testament*, 23.

12. Wright, *New Testament and the People of God*, 362.

13. Cuming, ed., *Apostolic Tradition of Hippolytus*.

14. Couratin, "Pre-history of the Liturgy."

have either a specific rite nor actual words (*ipsissima verba*) used within it during the era of the Jesus movement.

From the earliest and missionary days of the pre-Christendom church, we need to note that this "Jesus movement" accepted baptism, both as a uniting and common practice of marking an individual's journey into the communal and prophetic reign of God and their new identity in Christ, signified by the bestowal, through the ceremony itself, of the Holy Spirit.

The Sharing of Bread and Wine

There is no doubt that there exists an absolute historical connection between the sharing of bread and wine in the Upper Room narrative, as recorded in all four canonical Gospels, and what the later church began to describe as "the Mass," "the Eucharist," "Holy Communion," or "the Lord's Supper," and other appellations.[15] As the late Anglican liturgical scholar Cheslyn Jones wrote: "As we set out to assess the evidence for the [Eucharist] in the New Testament, our task seems delicate and difficult, yet very important . . . because we are not concerned with sacramental doctrine in general but with liturgical rites and practice, and . . . we have to rely on rather slender evidence."[16] "Slender" because what began as a shared meal between the earthly Jesus and his disciples, then witnessed to in just a handful of the apostolic writings (Matt 26:17–30; Mark 14:12–25; Luke 22:7–20; 1 Cor 11:23–25), has assumed huge significance in the life of the Jesus movement, consequent Christian community, and the life of the Christendom church.

What should be noted is that the core testimony to the life of that early missionary church is the Christian Bible, hampered and strengthened by successive translations. As a Galilean, Jesus of Nazareth would have spoken Aramaic for much of his public ministry. The New Testament was written in Greek, it was then translated into Latin, then the vernacular, during the Christendom era. In reality there are still in existence only fragments of those earliest writings, and what is printed in the various versions of the Bible can only ever be a paraphrase or a translation of what was written in Greek, then translated into Latin.

As previously explained, Aramaic was a language predominantly without verbs; it was also an oral rather than written language. So when Jesus lifted a loaf from the Upper Room table and said, "This, my body," or an earthenware cup, saying, "This, my blood," it is reasonable to imagine that the broken bread

---

15. Kreider, *Communion*, 19–98.

16. Jones et al., eds., *Study of Liturgy*, 188–89.

or poured-out wine symbolically portray Jesus' soon-to-be-broken body and spilled blood. What happened after that Last Supper in the Upper Room was initially an onward oral tradition. How much was it the discernment of the Gospel writers to create the pattern that Jesus "took, he blessed, he broke, he gave" to create the picture in the mind of later readers and listeners? Was this the Greek of the Gospel writers adopting the patterns described by Paul's earlier writings? Certainly by the formation and acceptance of the canon, those words were in the Greek and Latin texts of the Gospels.

But the implication of later theologians, from the medieval period forward, was that this four-action shape of "taking, blessing, breaking, sharing" was Jesus' intended pattern for all time, thus becoming an inalienable liturgical pattern for the subsequent church. Dom Gregory Dix explored these more fully in his seminal work in the last century.[17] This brings us back neatly to Couratin's thesis, outlined above, that the practices of the missionary church gained both credence and permanence as they were absorbed into the apostolic writings of the New Testament. What we are saying is that, recalling Jeremias's teaching, we can be fairly certain that we can recover the intention (*ipsissima vox*) of Jesus, but not always the actual words (*ipsissima verba*).[18] When and if the later definition of a sacrament requires the latter, we must be aware of the "slender" fragility of the biblical material in its onward communication and repeated translation.

This is instrumental when we approach what academically is presumed to be the earliest account of the Last Supper's shape in Paul's writing in the tenth and eleventh chapters of his first letter to the Corinthians. We cannot know in what kind of moment, theophany, or vision Paul "received that which I have given on to you, that on the night of his arrest, Jesus . . ." (1 Cor 11:23, our translation). It is consistent with the later Gospel accounts, as well as with the concept of the messianic banquet in Revelation.

This messianic banquet draws on ancient Hebrew imagery of the celebratory feast hosted by God on Mount Zion when the exile of the Jewish people is ended (Isa 25:11), an image which invites readers to enter into an "anamnestic" experience—that is, to understand themselves as invited to a banquet existing beyond time, one which incorporates all God's people from the past, the present, and the future.

Understanding the principle of anamnesis is at the core of interpreting what Jesus meant when he instructed his followers to eat and drink "in remembrance of me." He was not simply instructing them to think about him. Instead he was asking them to enter into a metaphorical "re-membering" of

17. Dix, *Shape of the Liturgy*.
18. Jeremias, *Eucharistic Words*.

- the development of liturgical rites for the sacraments.

These (and others) are concepts that have enriched Western civilization.

An important point to consider when assessing the impact of institutionalization on the church is how the understanding of how God works in the world changes. Within an imperial context, a faith which derives its power from the Spirit of a monotheistic God, and whose allegiance is to a man who died and was supposedly resurrected more than two hundred years before could be considered at least countercultural. By institutionalizing the Christian faith, the Romans were able also, to a certain extent, to "institutionalize" its basic beliefs. Authorizing the leaders to define particular beliefs gave the imperial powers the opportunity to rein in the difficult Christians, and to reframe the power of Jesus Christ and activity of the Holy Spirit within institutional terms. Thus the sacrament of baptism became synonymous with initiation of infants into the imperial (Christian) faith, only those authorized by the church were allowed to preside at the Eucharist, and the understanding of how the Holy Spirit works was relocated within the hierarchical structures of the church.

Just as there was a Romano-British Christianity, Christianity was already present and growing during the time of Constantine's changes across many of the empire's nations. One of the most influential Christians was Bishop Martin of Tours (ca. 320–397 CE); once a Gallic Roman soldier, he converted afterwards to trinitarian Christianity under the influence and tutelage of Hilary of Poitiers, before becoming a monk, hermit, then bishop who heavily influenced the rise and course of Western monasticism. What is important from this Anglo-French axis is to note that the "Jesus movement" of the first century had become quite widespread, with some similar patterns of life, leadership, and worship which took on the mantle of Christendom with some ease—creating both unity and uniformity.

The sacraments were both instrumental and integral to the life of the church—and its authority within society. What we must note is the triangular nature of the relationship between the church, its priesthood and the sacraments: the strength of each one relied on the strength of the other two.

The Historic Sacraments

In England the pre-Christendom church is often characterized by regionally autonomous Celtic Christian communities. From the second century CE, there was a growing Romano-British Christian presence in Britain[7] (see

---

7. Baring-Gould, *Ecclesiastica Celtica.*

above); in reality, they coexisted uneasily alongside each other. These tensions culminated in the Synod of Whitby in 664 CE. Until then itinerant monks gathered the faithful at the foot of Celtic crosses or folks would travel to abbeys and monastic houses. After Whitby's ruling by the Northumbrian king, the Roman patterns and practices were formally allowed to predominate. For example, Patrick was a Welsh herdsmen and a Romano-British Christian who was captured by pirates and transported in slavery to Ireland, where he later became both archbishop and known as "the apostle of all Ireland."

Christendom's development, and the establishment and use of sacraments as a way to ensure the conformity of belief, grew alongside the establishment of local "parish" church buildings. This latter pattern developed over the next six centuries, as people travelled to abbeys and minsters for "high days and holy days." Being noticeably seen in worship by the priests avoided ecclesiastical sanctions upon members of the congregation. Feudal Britain saw the owners of manorial estates design and construct their own church buildings, sometimes as chantries[8] or filial chapels of a nearby town's parish church if there was no local cathedral city. From the twelfth century, the parish structure developed rapidly, with priests becoming resident in parish communities, further strengthening the ecclesial power and enforcing conformity: including participation in the sacraments.

By the late English Middle Ages, attendance at Mass on certain days became compulsory, dissolution of marriage was banned, and the clergy were controlled in their orders and behavior after ordination. It could be argued that sacraments had become a matter of law and control. Christian marriage (which forbad divorce) was the perfect tool to control both aristocracy and merchants in their family life, and to manipulate the masses into compliance. For the clergy, ordination was given sacramental status, making its once-and-for-all action the perfect tool with which to control them. To reject, or even question, the sacraments, was seen as heretical, with a penalty of persecution or even death.[9]

An individual could not be legitimately married or ordained unless they had been baptized. As infant baptism became a rite of joining the Christendom church, it may no longer have been a matter of personal profession but one of corporate obedience by the parents to the life of the church. Justinian's principle had spilled over. If an individual was to have any formal life in society, with rights, perhaps a title or land, they had to have formally become a citizen and that meant being part of the Christian community—as indicated by baptism. Although paedo-baptism was practiced in the pre-Christendom

8. Kreider, *English Chantries.*

9. Southern, *Western Society.*

church, it became normative during this period, and dissenters from such practice were deemed heretical because they were shunning a "sacrament of the church." The adult-baptizing dissenters' logic ran that if Jesus as the Son of God acknowledged his need of baptism (by John) personally, how could any merely mortal human shun the practice?[10]

The church knew enough of Jesus' gracious command, "Follow me," to recognize that there must be a point at which an already baptized individual accepts responsibility to acknowledge the name of Christ. Without laboring this, there had to be a liturgical recognition of personal belief. It was only when someone was baptized that they could be given confirmation of their status as a Christian and permission to receive the bread and wine. By the time of the Norman Conquest (1066 CE), liturgical rites for the celebration of (what is often termed) Holy Communion were promulgated and recognized by Rome; these services were in Latin, which helped maintain both unity and uniformity.[11] To hold office, from monarch to merchant to monk, one had to be "in communion" with the Christendom church—in other words a law-abiding citizen. Thus felons, murderers, and even unruly kings could be excommunicated, effectively outlawing them from Christendom society. So, the sacrament known as the Mass, the Eucharist, or Holy Communion gained a canonical status.

Not all human wrongdoings merited excommunication. But there had to be a way in which the church could express its displeasure and exact some form of recompense from those whose faith fell short of the expected mark. This led to the sacrament of penance, in which a Christian privately confessed their sins to a priest, who would then demand a certain penitential response (i.e., penance) be made before the person could receive the Eucharist again. It became a matter of Christian obedience always to make one's confession and undertake penance prior to Mass, which held the laity under a further form of control by the priesthood.

But if all that was for this earthly life, being part of God's church must in the common mind have had heavenly benefits, too. So, certainly by the late Middle Ages, rites of passage were developed for the dying. As the rites continued to develop into their modern forms, they were known as "Extreme Unction," "Divine Unction," or the "Anointing of the Sick" or more loosely and colloquially as "the last rites." Historically, the Roman Catholic Church taught that a soul would not go to heaven unless the last rites had been administered, which would also include confession and *viaticum*—a final Eucharist. So, the

10. Hut, "Mystery of Baptism," 83–84.

11. Jones et al., eds., *Study of Liturgy*, 184–285.

logic ran, if someone's earthly misdemeanors caused excommunication, that person could not receive the last rites and so their soul would not go to heaven.

The Roman Catholic Council of Trent, which ran from 1545 until 1563, declared the following in its first canonical article:

> If any one saith, that the sacraments of the New Law were not all instituted by Jesus Christ, our Lord; or that they are more, or less, than seven, to wit, Baptism, Confirmation, the Eucharist, Penance, Extreme Unction, Order, and Matrimony; or even that any one of these seven is not truly and properly a sacrament; let him be *anathema*.[12]

This had been the case for generations as the Roman Catholic Church had exerted its control over "the faithful" but now it was overtly stated. Why? Because far more than dissent had occurred: Europe was already in the grip of the Reformation. If the Catholic Church was to regain its previous influence over the people, it needed to reassert itself and it used all seven sacraments to wield that power.

With hindsight, it is simplistic—but almost correct—to impute entirely different motives for the mainland continental Reformation of Luther, Zwingli, and Calvin and that of Henry VIII in England. Henry was objecting to the papal and sacramental control that decreed that marriage was indissoluble, when Henry wished to annul his marriage and thus effectively to divorce Catherine of Aragon to marry Anne Boleyn.[13] The English Reformation was political, pitting the power of the English monarch against the ultramontane (literally "over the mountains") authority of Rome. The Continental Reformers were far more spiritually minded, wanting the development of regional communions, using vernacular liturgies and Scripture while rejecting the sacramental and other excesses of a papal-driven Christendom church. These Reformers wanted to put Jesus and the teaching of biblical faith back into the hands and lives of people.[14] Yet both of these mainstream Reformations began a centuries-long process of re-evaluating the nature, number, and power of the sacraments, as we shall discover in more detail in forthcoming pages.

However, it was the continental Radical Reformers, predominantly the sixteenth-century Anabaptists who (like St. Francis two centuries before them) saw that Jesus-shaped discipleship was far more alternative, countercultural, and radical than to be constrained in a sacramental church controlled

---

12. Santa, *Essential Catholic Handbook*, ix.

13. Haugaard, *Elizabeth and the English Reformation*.

14. Lau and Bizer, *Reformation in Germany*.

by priests, instead of by the gathered people of God.[15] A major aspect of this was their belief that the Holy Spirit was at work in each of their lives, not just within the institution of the church. Basing their corporate life and worship forms on a new reading of the Bible, they began to model Christian living with a level of freedom unheard of within the church at that time.

Anabaptism placed Jesus firmly back at the center of faithful discipleship and it was his earthly teaching and alternative pattern of open eating together and radical egalitarianism that was and is the Anabaptists' declared norm for all Christians. They were called ana-baptists because they believed that a consenting adult must profess activist faith in Jesus prior to baptism; accordingly, they were deemed to be *wiedertaufer* (Ger.), *doopgezinde* (Dutch), or ana-baptists, which meant they were re-baptizers. Such practice was against Christendom and specifically Roman Catholic doctrine and led to Anabaptists' excommunication and persecution unto death.[16]

Two key factors should be noted here:

- Some heavily persecuted Anabaptists from the Netherlands escaped to London and the East Anglian region of England. The Anabaptists were despised by the nascent Anglican Church, being condemned in its defining Thirty-Nine Articles. So after a number of Anabaptists were martyred by burning at Smithfield, London, many joined the "underground" neo-congregationalist Brownist movement. Lest we forget, those Brownist Christians were Puritans and it was from among their number that the Pilgrim Fathers were gathered and sailed to the American colonies taking their style of Christianity with them—as well as their desire for a separation of church and state.[17]

- The above-mentioned Council of Trent was part of the Roman Catholic Church's reaction and resistance to the various forms of Reformation. Traditionally, church historians prefer to call this whole response the Counter-Reformation.

In one sense, the Church of England suddenly arrived by fiat and decision of Henry VIII, and had to decide quickly how to move from simply being the "English Catholic Church" to an entity in its own right. So, the Church of England (which historically has led the global Anglican Communion since then) attempted to hold a diverse position. It accepted that baptism and Holy Communion are two central and biblical sacraments. But there were many,

---

15. Francis, *Anabaptism.*

16. Murray, *Naked Anabaptist.*

17. Francis, *Anabaptism.*

among its more catholic-oriented members, who wanted it to do far more than acknowledge that the other five historic sacraments were "valid expressions of the faith." Historic Anglican wrestling about sacraments since the Reformation led to it becoming a "broad church," not easily tolerant of other views, and has set an agenda to the present day.

Unlike contemporary liberal Quakerism (now predominantly theocentric rather than christocentric), early to mid-seventeenth-century Quakers built their call and proclamation around Jesus, his pacifist teaching, and radical egalitarianism, whilst developing non-sacramental communities expressing a priesthood of all believers (1 Pet).[18]

The original eighteenth-century Methodist movement in England centered its revivalist preaching around the person, work, and teaching of Jesus Christ, creating an ecclesiology in which preaching and gathering in small study groups assumed more importance than the sacraments had in its "spawning Anglican parent."[19] During the twentieth century, the role of the Methodist Sacramental Fellowship should not be underestimated in its connexional lobbying and personal influence of many good scholars, fine liturgists, and faithful congregants in reaffirming their Anglican sacramental heritage and its importance in shaping ongoing Methodism.

Nineteenth-century Restorationism gave rise to the Churches of Christ and the Plymouth Brethren; both these movements utilized the pattern, life, and teaching of the earthly Jesus as the central core of their ecclesial life and theology (although the Brethren still often "forget" Jesus' inclusion of women as equals).[20]

In the twentieth century it was through liberation theology that the shift back to a Jesus-at-the-center theology started to take root, changing the focus in many developing Roman Catholic communities from sacrament-based "churches" to lay-led neighborhood "base ecclesial communities." Through their peasant art[21] and open discussion of the Gospels' imperatives in the favelas, where everyone contributed, these faithful base church communities challenged Christendom Christology into fundamental change.[22] Changes in sacramental practice reflected the prioritizing of inclusion and welcome over classical doctrinal practices.[23]

---

18. Dandelion, *Quakers.*

19. Stutzmann, *Recovering the Love Feast.*

20. Robinson, *Shattered Cross.*

21. Scharper and Scharper, *Gospel in Art.*

22. Sobrino, *Christology.*

23. Boff and Boff, *Introducing Liberation Theology.*

However, it has been the rise of the Pentecostal movement that has posed the starkest challenge to sacramental theology and practice in the last fifty years. Just as the Radical Reformers of the sixteenth century rediscovered the power of the Holy Spirit at work in the everyday, so the Pentecostals—as their name suggests—focus on the power of the Holy Spirit to work, both individually and corporately, through their worship life.

Like the Anabaptists, the Pentecostal tradition—which itself is wide, varied, and becoming globally more powerful—has moved away from the notion of formal "sacraments." Pentecostals have no requirement for a priesthood to authorize Spirit-led activities and practices within the context of their worship. Basing their community formation on the Ephesians model, Pentecostal communities tend to appoint those recognized for their gifts of apostolic thought, gifts of prophecy, evangelism, pastoring, and teaching. In addition glossolalia—the act of speaking in tongues with interpretation—is highly regarded as a practice by which God the Holy Spirit becomes present within the gathering. It is clear that while glossolalia is not regarded a sacrament, as a corporate activity, a "moment of grace" brought about through the in-breaking of God's holiness, it can be argued that speaking in tongues with interpretation could be considered sacramental.

Post-Christendom Has Already Arrived . . .

What radical non-Christendom movements, liberation theology, and the Pentecostal movement demonstrate is how a Jesus-at-the-center theology challenges ecclesiocentric theology. The radical shift from an understanding of the church as an institution, to being communities of individual believers with the person of Jesus as faith's compass point and the Holy Spirit as an active participant, enables a less rigid approach to the sacraments. The impact of liberation theology, then Pentecostalism, on the world church has been immense. This desacralizing of the church with a formal priesthood has created a seedbed, across Latin America and Africa, for the influx, establishment, and growth of Pentecostal congregations, with their congregational autonomy and preference for ordinances, not sacraments.[24]

As the Christendom age fades away, and many North American, mainland European, Irish, and British denominations struggle to maintain traditions and practices perceived as outdated and irrelevant, the church as a Jesus-centered community is beginning to rediscover itself. Both within formal church settings, and through myriad Jesus-following communities

---

24. Martin, *Forgotten Revolution.*

springing up, believers are experimenting in new ways of worshiping, living a life of discipleship, and engaging in what might be called sacramental practices.

So our next chapter picks up on this "after Christendom" challenge, before we undertake a section of a series of shorter chapters, each exploring how some other practices may be considered as sacramental. But should they be called sacraments?

4

The Challenge of Post-Christendom

Since the turn of the century, there has been a growing body of evidence in the United Kingdom suggesting a rise in the numbers of people describing themselves as "spiritual but not religious."[1] More recently the Barna Group has conducted extensive research that demonstrates that this is also so in the United States.[2] It seems that to be described as religious by others can be perceived as an insult, implying that one is in thrall to an institutionalized way of religious adherence with little or no personal right to question nor be a seeker of truth for oneself. Thus the historic Christian church is represented as the purveyor of such religion, and the inherited (our preferred term) denominations such as the Roman Catholic, Anglican, Methodist, and Baptist Churches are regarded as such.

Today postmodernism is considered not as much a challenging new concept as a given, a period marking the end of the modern era and the start of a new one yet to be named.[3] Although the world is viewed by those studying both postmodernism and post-Christendom in similar ways, the two are not coterminous. While postmodernists understand the "big stories" of faith traditions—technically known as metanarratives—to be allegorical (e.g., containing creation myths), post-Christendom theologians and practitioners are endeavoring to find new ways to offer opportunities to discover a faith in Jesus Christ and to experience Christian community for themselves.

As modernism, and its obsession with scientific fact, fades into the past, commentators such as the populist-but-academic atheist Richard Dawkins,

1. Heelas and Woodhead, *Spiritual Revolution*.
2. https://www.barna.com/research/meet-spiritual-not-religious/.
3. Eagleton, *Illusions of Post-Modernism*.

continue to cling to a scientific, rather than religious, worldview or meta-narrative.[4] Others take this further, pointing to an increasing distrust of the religious metanarratives that have sustained and supported society's polities, such as Christendom, for centuries. They point out that distrust extends over the power of religious rites and rituals (such as sacraments) to exercise a real influence over individuals. The Israeli historian and social commentator Noah Yuval Harari, in his cogent writings[5] and broadcast work, is probably currently the best-known globally influential voice, implying that the failure of Christendom as well as the demise of Christianity and other world faiths are leading towards more widespread skeptical humanism. Others like the Dutch primatologist Frans de Waal use such postmodern scientific thought and processes to explain why religion, and even spiritual experience, is not necessary for postmodern humanity. In his *The Bonobo and the Atheist*, de Waal advances the theory that morals are a matter of primate evolution and are not part of any received metanarrative of faith or part of a perceived spirituality from above;[6] therefore, in his thought, religion is a myth that uses its practices (including the sacraments) to control its adherents.

Contrast these propositions with those of scholars such as the Mennonite John D. Rempel, who describes the practices of the Christian faith as a way of "clothing God's transcendence in immanence."[7] It is far more rewarding to align oneself with the eloquence of Rempel's writing in *Recapturing an Enchanted World*, than to adhere to the message of the tolling bell of sociologists Steve Bruce or Callum Brown.[8] We seek instead to reaffirm our belief in an orthodox trinitarian Christian faith, at the same time *knowing* that we must question the ways in which the institutional church has wielded power and authority—often to the detriment of others' individual beliefs.

The transition from modernism towards postmodernism and from Christendom to post-Christendom can be characterized by the priority experience is taking over knowledge. Once again we turn to Rempel, who asserts that:

> The realm of the incarnational and sacramental can be grasped only where there is openness to the human capacity for imaginative as well as rational perception. The metaphorical imagination

---

4. Dawkins, *God Delusion.*

5. Harari, *Sapiens*; Harari, *Homo Deus*; Harari, *21 Lessons.*

6. de Waal, *Bonobo.*

7. Rempel, *Recapturing*, 36.

8. Brown, *Death of Christian Britain*; Bruce, *God is Dead.*

is at home in the realm of spirit; it apprehends truth that would otherwise be inaccessible to us.[9]

And the only way to access this, affirms Rempel, is through faith. "After Christendom"/"post Christendom" faith, in its emphasis of experience over knowledge, enables a fluidity of "practice" rather than rigid conformity to a system. It becomes more important to experience something than to actually have to describe every jot and tittle of its instruction manual. This is why the broader debate about sacraments (of which this book is part) is so important. The sacraments are to be experienced and not just talked or taught about without reference to how they change and transform the human heart and soul. Our personal faith makes us aware of how and why involvement in sacramental activity, with like-minded others, gives us an identity "in Christ" and enriches our life in God. We want others to have that experience.

"We Want to See Jesus . . ."

As early as the first century in Galilee, seekers wanted to see, therefore encounter and experience Jesus (John 12:21); knowledge about him was not enough. It does not require a huge amount of searching on the internet today to discover that this is still so. The sheer number of articles and posts, covering issues as varied as what Jesus looked like, whether he really did rise from the dead, and what his teachings mean today, highlights the continued fascination with the person of Jesus Christ. The number of artistic depictions, spiritual tomes, and expressions of Jesus, or of Christian believing or the church through the ages, provide enough historical evidence to demonstrate that interest in the life and voice of Jesus has never diminished.

According to Mark, the Gospel writer, fascination with Jesus was present among his contemporaries, from the lowliest leper to the royal elite. When Herod asks who this Jesus of Nazareth could possibly be, the respondents compare him with the greatest prophets and with John the Baptist.[10] Such comparisons tell us much about how Jesus was viewed in his own time. He provided a powerful voice on behalf of the poor and oppressed, as well as healing the sick and preaching acceptance for those on the margins of society. The redemption and reconciliation he promised, and later demonstrated through his death and resurrection, would hardly have suited a king who, as a vassal of the Romans, enjoyed all the privileges of imperial power without having to

---

9. Rempel, *Recapturing*, 53.

10. Myers, *Binding*.

display any signs of spiritual enlightenment. We suggest that the same might be said of those wielding power around the world today.

If the Christian community, and individual believers within it, know that their true and fullest identity is "in Christ," it is a natural assumption to expect that this will also be their desire for others who do not yet share that best and most human of spiritual experiences. Helping people to answer the questions, "Who am I?" and "Who are we?' are questions of identity. They are in part answered by what we do (often together) to give shape to our lives. For those "in Christ," some of the key things we share as part of our faith are things most easily described as sacramental. What we are suggesting is that any discussion of the sacraments is necessarily concerned with Christian identity, because:

- our sacramental practice is always set within a tradition and we almost certainly associate ourselves with (a) specific Christian tradition(s);

- the earliest Christians marked themselves out by the radical nature of their sacramental practices;

- we can see how the sacraments have been used in history as tools of control, enforcing colonial identity; and

- how we identify ourselves in Christ, or as Jesus-followers is associated with how we encounter the divine within the mundane.

As writers, ministers or presbyters,[11] and theologians, we can understand how the sacraments have become vital touchstones for the inherited denominations. At their best, sharing in a communal, therefore a re-membering and reuniting moment and activity, creatively molds one's discipleship. This enables the believers (and other participants) to share a life-giving experience of God. But at its most mundane, poor teaching about sacraments, as well as an enforced loyalty or blind adherence to their bland practice, creates a stumbling block to faith. Members of inherited denominations are not always good, or even honest, about how their identity is perceived—whether that is spiritual or religious.

With all this in mind we return to the question posed in the introduction to this chapter: if more than half the British population do not identify as Christian (active churchgoers are less than 6 percent of the population),[12] then what do the sacraments mean in Britain today? How does the historical understanding of sacramentality and practice need to be reviewed or changed for the twenty-first century? And how does the influence of the growing tide

11. A globally used ecumenical term (an alternative to "clergy") to encompass priests, ministers, pastors, etc.

12. Faith Survey, "Christianity in the UK."

However, before we move into that, we need to explain the way in which we "measure" the hows, whys, and whethers of these encounters called "sacraments."

5

"Sacrament," "*Mysterion*," "Ordinance," or Something Else?

From the discussion so far it is clear that there is no easy way to define a sacrament and, while several definitions exist, no adequate set of criteria has been developed against which one can measure the extent to which a ritual or practice is "a sacrament" or "sacramental."

There has been no time in church history when all Christians have been able to agree what a "sacrament" is, or even how many there should be; while there are other traditions who have, throughout their history, been able to live entirely without them. Still others have instituted "ordinances," probably best described as activities that symbolize or embody the activity of God through Christ in the world.

The term *sacrament* comes from the Latin word meaning "solemn oath" or "sacred vow." It was used to describe the tattoo Roman soldiers had when they pledged their allegiance to their unit—a signifier of a covenant never to be broken, even beyond death.[1] The Greek equivalent, *mysterion*, is defined as one might expect—a ritual that invokes the covenantal presence of a God whose being is a mystery beyond human comprehension. A third possibility is the Russian word таинство—transliterated into English as *tainstvo*. Although it is translated into English as "sacrament," it reflects the Orthodox Church's understanding of sacrament: a sacred practice through which the participant enters into the mystery of the incarnation through a set of required words and actions.

One approach to setting the criteria against which a sacrament is to be measured is, first, to define it; then, second, tease out the definition's contents.

---

1. Calvin, *Institutes*, XIV.13, 1288; cf. Sahi, "Sacred Space," 132–33.

One definition might be this: "A sacrament is a particular activity or rite enacted between individuals within the context of a faith community. Using agreed symbols, liturgy (words) and actions, its principal aim is to invoke an awareness of the presence of God, and to convey a particular spiritual idea or experience through the participation of those present." While this might seem straightforward, in reality it contains a number of different clauses, each of which presupposes a number of interdependent complex interactions between:

- the nature, purpose, and function of the rite;
- the identities of those present;
- the language and symbols used; and
- the expectation of how God will be experienced through its enacting.

How these are to be understood is far from clear; and the way in which each of the clauses will be interpreted will vary for each reader according to a variety of factors, such as personal religious influences and the corporate context within which the activity is set.

Underpinning Our Approach

To clarify, the definition presupposes that:

1. A sacrament is a particular activity or rite enacted between individuals with a common understanding of shared *identity*;

2. It is enacted within the *context* of a faith community;

3. Its principal aim is to invoke an awareness of or enter into the *covenant* presence of God;

4. Its purpose is to convey a particular spiritual idea or experience through the participation of those present, one relating specifically to their *tradition*;

5. It is enacted using an agreed set of *symbols*, liturgy (words), and actions.

What exactly those participating understand to be taking place is influenced by how they make meaning and create order within their own faith context.

Social psychologists J. Peter Burke and Jane Stets, in their book *Identity Theory*, suggest that individuals use language, signs, symbols, and gestures to make meaning and create order.[2] These meanings must be identified, named, and shared in order for a successful interaction to take place. Certain categories, concepts, labels, and symbols provide the means to "define the situation." Each designation has little meaning by itself, but put together they produce a context.[3] Burke and Stets illustrate this with the example of a conversation between a sales consultant, a sales manager, and an accountant. All three actors in the encounter will have common definitions of each person's role in the company and what each will be expected to contribute. Each would be free to reject these expectations, but by token of their shared context, they engage in behaviors that reinforce it. Those behaviors include the language they utilize and gestures they use. Although the three actors in the exchange might have slightly different purposes and expect different outcomes, it is highly likely that the interaction will prove successful because of their myriad shared understandings.

At this point, we should make clear that "sacrament" and "ritual" are not coterminous. Rituals can vary from the mundane to the sacred; walking the dog every morning and always attending a midweek, quiet Communion are very different forms of ritual. Theory about ritual is sometimes relegated to the activity of religious practice while the more adept sociologists always affirm ritual is also about our very human but everyday routines.[4]

In his short theological work *Holy Trinity, Perfect Community*, Leonardo Boff suggests similarly that how people understand the world to be depends on how they make meaning: "History . . . has meaning, and meanings are created within it alongside the persistence of existential and collective absurdities. Even so, it is mysteriously inhabited by the august mystery of the Father, the Son and the Holy Spirit . . . This mystery becomes embodied in history, because it is organized in groups and communities."[5] Therefore, communities in turn assume the elements of each age, so that the church has as many faces as the incarnations it has undergone throughout history.

Boff states that God, who is "a boundless mystery," can be seen in every element of human society and its associated interactions. He further states that "The Blessed Trinity is a sacramental mystery. In other words, it is something that appears in many signs, that can always be known; yet our effort to know never ends."[6] This mystery, human-divine encounter, or "moment of grace" as it might be described, is something towards which humankind has

2. Burke and Stets, *Identity Theory*.

3. Burke and Stets, *Identity Theory*, 13–15.

4. E.g., Bell, *Ritual*.

5. Boff, *Holy Trinity*.

6. Boff, *Holy Trinity*, 115.

FIGURE 1

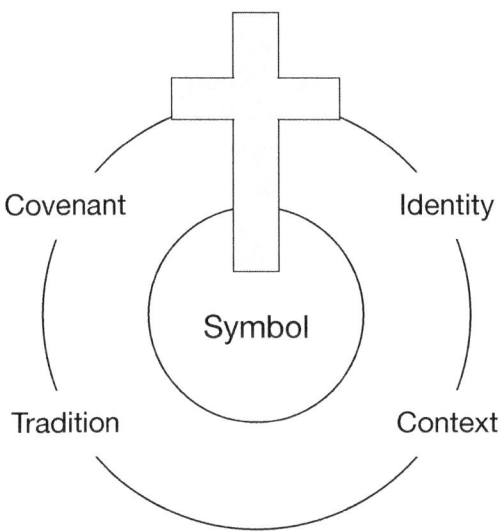

It might seem obvious, but is worth stating explicitly, that the difference between the Jewish and Christian perception of what was taking place in these "moments of grace" was the presence, among those gathered, of God the Father, Son, and Holy Spirit.

In the following chapters we will explore how this typology can be used to examine how sacramental praxis has developed throughout church history. However, it seems pertinent to begin by considering the framework in the context of the most current sacramental issue at the time of writing: whether the Eucharist remains efficacious, or indeed valid, when celebrated using live streaming or a recorded service during a lockdown situation.

Celebrating the Eucharist during the COVID-19 Pandemic

At the time of writing this paragraph, it is Holy Week, 2020. In nations across the world entire populations have become subject to stringent, sometimes statutory restrictions, curtailing freedom of movement and banning public or private gatherings. Fact has become stranger than fiction. Regardless of tradition, context, identity, or understanding of how the sacraments relate to a human-divine encounter with the covenant God, the challenges to the church in its myriad manifestations have been numerous.

While the use of technology has enabled "communities of faith" to relate on a daily basis, and to "gather" online, those elements we have identified as essential to sacramental practice have been radically challenged or, in some cases, become entirely absent. For some it has been possible to take a pragmatic view and "make the best of it"—inviting people to take bread and wine in their homes while participating in a streamed service or, in the case of Pope Francis, authorizing the use of alternative methods. For other Christians, whose sacramental identity is deeply embedded in the physicality of the act itself, this has been a time of profound grief. As one English clergyperson commented on their Facebook page: "I have just watched the live streaming of the Archbishop of Canterbury's Palm Sunday Eucharist. And I find myself wondering, what's the point?"

As we stated at the outset, whether it be through signs, symbols, words, or actions, God breaks into the lives of individuals and Christian communities through the rituals, ordinances, or other practices considered sacramental within corporately identified traditions. Set within this understanding of the sacraments, it is easy to see how the removal of one or more accepted elements necessarily impacts on the efficacy of the act itself:

- If one is isolated from the rest of the body of Christ;

- If the symbols which act as signifiers are absent;

- If one's sacramental practice is deeply enmeshed with the importance of place and that place is locked shut, then how does one participate in a meaningful way?

During this Holy Week the sharing in the forsakenness of the cross is taking on a new resonance as the coronavirus continues to spread, and the ability of Christians to partake in those rituals that make their covenant God real to them is denied.

It is not for two authors to dictate how, or indeed whether, altered sacramental practices in differing traditions can maintain authenticity. Rather, we would like to suggest that the above framework could prove useful in enabling theologians, practitioners, and practicing Christians across the globe to identify why they have responded in the way they have to the sacramental challenges presented by coronavirus, and ultimately its aftermath. In doing so we hope that a new atmosphere of openness might prevail, as the churches find new ways of being the body of Christ in the post-COVID-19 world.

By combining identity theory with an analysis of human-divine encounter in the Hebrew Scriptures and very early Christian experience, we are now equipped with a framework through which to explore how sacramental praxis has developed throughout church history. We begin with a closer look at the dominical sacraments, before going on to explore the extent to which other rituals and practices, some of which have been defined as "sacraments" or "ordinances," might be described as "sacramental" or "moments of grace."

Part Two

Encountering God
in Differing Christian Traditions

6

Baptism and Eucharist

My (Janet's) abiding memory of being a member of an emerging church community in the early 2000s is the sharing of bread and wine with a whole host of Christians from very different traditions. Roman Catholics, Quakers, and Methodists joined with Anglicans, Baptists, and "we're not sures," to share a common cup and loaf of bread in Jesus' name.

I don't think any of us, theologically trained or not, could deny the anamnetic nature of the experience we shared. As we ate and drank, Christ became present for each of us in that room, and we became one "in Christ."

It wasn't a sacrament . . . or at least it wasn't recognized as one by the Church of England, who sponsored the Church Army Officer leading it. He wasn't ordained, the bread and wine weren't consecrated, no epiclesis (the formal words invoking the activity of the Holy Spirit) was said. And yet . . .

There is an old British joke that the last seven words of the church will be: "We've never done it like that before." In moving into this book's second part, we need to ask, "What is it that makes a particular in-breaking of God's holiness a sacrament?" It is not simply tradition—"because we have always done it like that" or "it's always been called a sacrament"—which makes that activity sacramental or even a sacrament.

We have already reaffirmed that there was no point in Christian history at which all communions, traditions, movement, or parties were in unanimous agreement about which if any were sacraments and, if so, how many there were. So, why start to pretend now that such accord ever existed? However, we do believe that it is the absolute right of every communion, inherited denomination, and contemporary Christian community to be self-determining about the issue of sacraments and their number. What is important is that they have discerned a common mind about what is sacramental, what a sacrament is, and how many they observe, while they are able to say what objective criteria they have used for such discernment—as we have done in the preceding chapter.

What we are clear about is that sacraments are part of the church's mission. We are not alone in this. We acknowledge both the encouraging work in North America of Lizette Larson-Miller, an Episcopal priest, writer, and academic theologian, and that of John Rempel, a Mennonite pastor and liturgical theologian, in creatively helping foster the North American "sacraments debate."

Larson-Miller suggests that sacramental theology, like Christianity, is constantly developing and evolving. Although they have ancient scriptural and revelatory foundations, human imagination and experience have continued to combine to influence the way the sacraments are understood and practiced.[1] Like us she identifies a seminal statement made by Rowan Williams, then Archbishop of Canterbury:

> Church is not primarily an event in which we do something, think something, feel something, it is being together in a situation where we trust God to do something and to change us . . . One of the challenges of being church . . . is how to make this movement from what we do to what God does; how to create an environment in which church can happen in the fullest sense, with the sacramental life flowing through as a sign and channel of God's action.[2]

So in our desire to nurture further debate about sacraments, we are not trying to say "this is" and "that is not" a sacrament in each chapter. We have acknowledged the expressions of genuine pain from those who understand the sacraments in this way during the COVID-19 months. We want instead to explore whether "moments of grace," which might be described as sacramental, might helpfully be incorporated into sacramental praxis after Christendom.

Baptism

Any discussion on the topic of baptism as a sacrament must acknowledge that the term *baptism* encompasses two very different types of activities. As we have already stated, both types—believers' and infant baptism—serve the purpose of enabling the participant to enter into the *covenant* presence of God. The ceremony must be enacted within the *context* of a faith community with

1. Larson-Miller, *Sacramentality Revisited*, 75–77.
2. Larson-Miller, *Sacramentality Revisited*, 77.

a shared *identity*, using an agreed set of *symbols*, liturgy (words), and actions. However, the way in which this is outworked and the theology which underpins the two very different practices varies greatly according to the *tradition* of the Christian community within which it takes place. James Gray writes that "for baptism to be a sacrament, it must take place within the corporate worship of a gathered church. It requires not only the action of God and the intentionality of the baptismal candidate and their sponsors, but also the support, welcome and promised nurture of that gathered congregation."[3] However, this understanding is very different from that held in a typical English parish church, where clergy are obliged to baptize any candidate, infant or adult, as part of their civic duty, providing the candidates have not been baptized before.

It is therefore necessary first to separate the two different types of baptism to explore their efficacy as sacramental moments within the individual and corporate lives of Christian communities.

Can Infant Baptism be Regarded as a Sacrament?

We have already seen that infant baptism as a sacramental practice has roots early in the Christendom era, and has, in most traditions, been accepted as a means of initiation into the church. Indeed, Calvin went as far as to say it has its roots within the Judaic practice of circumcision.[4] However, there is scant biblical evidence to support this, and church fathers' references to "household baptisms" *may* have included children, although it is by no means certain. Anecdotal evidence from urban parish-based colleagues suggests that requests for infant baptisms are falling sharply and the actual number conducted is even fewer, while in rural areas the "baby's christening" is as much about "wetting the baby's head" (celebrating their safe arrival, with a family party) as it is about promising to actually bring them up in the life of the church. In the UK, infant baptisms are often called "christenings," and are viewed as naming ceremonies, the name being derived from the term "Christ-namings."

In our ministries both authors have, in common with the practice of the Anglican mission-educator Robin Green, encouraged inquiring parents and representative congregants to explore together (over weeks, even months) what they commonly believe takes place during the sacramental moment of baptism *before* arranging the ceremony for a particular infant.[5] As United Re-

3. Gray, *Studies in Baptism*.
4. Calvin, *Institutes*.
5. Green, *Only Connect*, 51–65.

formed Church ministers it is then left to our conscience whether we conduct the baptism or arrange for another suitably qualified individual to perform the ceremony. Whichever is the case, it is only when the promises of the gathered congregation and the intentions of the parents fully come together that the sacramental moment takes on its greatest meaning. For baptism to be a sacrament, it must take place within the corporate worship of the gathered church, who also make promises of faith as do the parents (in infant baptisms) and godparents (i.e., sponsors) to bring the child up in "the faith of the Gospel and the fellowship of the Church."[6]

Conscious of our learning from Anabaptist and other believers' baptism traditions,[7] we have always encouraged parents to consider (prayerfully if they are committedly Christian) a "Service of Thanksgiving for Childbirth and their Dedication to be Christian Parents." Parents must also consider that, if they opt for infant baptism, they might deny their child's right to be baptized later as a believer. Orthodox theology teaches that Christian baptism may only be undertaken once in a person's lifetime.

Our respective ministries have revealed differing stances over the decades among those inquiring about infant baptism. In two particularly highly secularized urban areas, one of us experienced wider family pressures upon new parents (for the sake of social conformity?) to promise before God that they will "bring the child up in the faith of the Gospel and the fellowship of the Church"[8] when their intention afterwards was blatantly not to do so. One family even publicly refused the church's gift of a Bible. Another occasion yielded the request for their Muslim neighbors to be the child's godparents.

Early in the twenty-first century, new parents seem more resistant to social pressure from their own parents and grandparents just to have the child "christened" (they rarely use the term "baptized"). However, the pressure is still created by church schools in England's state education sector demanding that both a baptismal certificate and evidence of churchgoing is an entry requirement for a child to be considered. It is valid to question the extent to which, if an action of the state requires a liturgical rite of the church, it can really be sacramental in nature, or indeed a "moment of grace."

It is certainly the intention of those administering infant baptism to require the declared and committed Christian faith of those bringing the child for baptism *and* all godparents, and for these promises to be relied upon. However, experience demonstrates this is not always the case. Add in the historic-to-current practice of royalty, high society, or celebrity families

---

6. United Reformed Church, "Baptism of Children," 32.

7. Durnbaugh, *Believers' Church.*

8. United Reformed Church, "Baptism of Children," 32.

requesting private baptismal ceremonies away from the corporate worship of the local, gathered church, then both the church's promises of support and the intentionality is lost. Again, one may question the extent to which these are "moments of grace."

The practice of baptizing infants was declared to be necessary when our denomination, the United Reformed Church in Great Britain (which had been formed in 1972 from a union of the Presbyterian and Congregational Churches) undertook its second national union, joining with the Churches of Christ in 1981. The Churches of Christ held to an Anabaptist polity.[9] However, a key factor in the union was the statement that *every* local congregation teach that, universally, both infant *and* believers' baptism are acceptable. This stance used background documents from the union schemes of the ecumenical Churches of North and South India, in order to maintain a globally acceptable stance.

In recent years both authors have found an increasing number of inquiring parents requesting naming ceremonies. We have conducted them, often with the use of symbols but not water, and often in nonliturgical settings. To spend time exploring with parents of infants what they wish to say and to celebrate (learning from Green's methodology[10]), can often lead to new expressions of gathering, liturgy, and meaningful responses. These occasions have often been moments of the in-breaking of God's holiness—but not in orthodox, sacramental ways. In a post-Christendom period, when beliefs are more vaguely held and the story of Jesus broadly unknown, such ceremonies, whether they be considered sacramental or not, will become more common— and perhaps more fitting. It will be for congregations—and their ministers or presbyters—to explore for themselves whether a rite for a new baby is a fitting way of opening the door to heaven for the child and their parents, and whether or not this might be considered a sacramental moment in the life of their faith community.

Believers' baptism

Andrew recalls childhood missionary rallies where Kodachrome slides showed indigenous Africans or south Asians lining up on a riverbank, as their

---

9. As stated previously, Anabaptists were a major part of the sixteenth century's Radical Reformation and now its dominant movement, in its various expressions. They believe in a clear separation of church and state, recognizing that the local congregation is a covenant community of adult professed believers, leading them to totally reject paedobaptism. Therefore an adult wishing to join an Anabaptist-styled congregation would have to be baptized as an adult, professing believer.

10. Green, *Only Connect*, 51–65.

fellow villagers looked on. Those who had accepted Christian faith went down into the water, were baptized by immersion, and came up onto the other bank, where they received a clean white shirt or dress to witness to the purity of God's moment. The occasional presence of guards in the river with large sticks to ward off crocodiles gave a frisson to the acknowledged dying-and-rising-with-Christ theology.

Andrew was baptized as a teenage believer. Janet has always wished she had been, her parents having chosen to have her baptized as a baby. Janet has baptized adults in the river on the edge of town and blessed babies at football clubs and garden parties. Andrew has led the immersive baptism of believers in tidal Iona Sound (Scotland), the Sea of Galilee, the Aegean, French rivers, and in other waters, as well as in grand church buildings and back-street chapels. On the occasion of each baptism, the gathered community of believers, family, and friends were called to witness the commitment being made. In this dying and rising (Rom 6), the believer was declaring Jesus as Lord of all and as personal savior while becoming incorporated into the "body of Christ" (Rom 12; Col 1). Witnessing a believer's baptism on a steep South American favela's dirt road, patrolled by guerrilla death squads, when the baptism was celebrated using precious drinking water poured over the new Christian from a bucket, gave Andrew cause to reject what seemed to him the "sanitization" of baptism in the Western church.

The teachings about Christian identity in the earliest missionary writings of the Christian church were a necessary encouragement to those baptized in the first century onward who were martyred for their faith in Jesus of Nazareth. Martyrdom continues in every century—even in allegedly Christian countries. Many of the sixteenth-century Anabaptists who chose to be (re-) baptized as believers found themselves persecuted and martyred.[11] It is popularly quoted that more Christians were martyred in the twentieth century than the total from the preceding nineteen Common Era centuries.[12] North Africa was a Christian region until Islamic expansionism bloodily swept Christianity away. Post-Christendom Westernized nations face fresh challenges to their Christian status from several directions. No one should ignore Pauline dying-and-rising-with-Christ theology and sacraments that symbolize the potential implications of those challenges.

From the second century, the newly baptized were anointed with the oil of chrism—essentially myrrh, a spice used to preserve bodies after death. In the Eastern/Orthodox tradition, this was known as "chrismation" and regarded as the second initiatory sacrament, with baptism as the first and Divine

11. Snyder, *Anabaptist History.*

12. Boyarin, *Dying for God*, 93.

Eucharist as the third. Chrismation was also used as a sign that believers in Jesus are sealed with the gift of the Holy Spirit to enrich and endow both discipleship and personal ministry. Contemporarily, Anglicans, Lutherans, Roman Catholics, and the Orthodox Churches, as well some more radical, more recent, fresh expressions of Christian community, still frequently use anointing with oil, normally at the time of confirmation or believers' baptism, to symbolize becoming "sealed with the Spirit."[13]

Christendom values meant that, once infants were baptized and therefore enlisted into the church, they were taught to conform and behave as Christians. Ultimately this meant declaring belief in Christ, but in medieval and early modern times, there was also a very real sense in which following Jesus meant renouncing the evil powers that people believed to be present in the world. There was a significant amount of activity among the laity in attempting to ward off these evil spirits. Baptismal water was "jealously guarded against lay misuse or contamination."[14] Generally speaking, medieval peasants were baptized as infants (possibly because of the superstitious view that, if they were not, they would go to hell). Would they have had the time to undergo teenage preparation for confirmation when they were vital laborers? It is difficult to envisage the medieval mind-set when it came to faith and belief. There was no division of sacred and secular, and the liturgical year was marked in a cycle which had as much to do with nature and astrology as the life, death, and resurrection of Christ. With saints and "holy days" (holidays) of obligation—when folk went to the grandest buildings around for worship, surrounded by icons, statues, stained glass, sacred paintings and murals, promenading morality plays, and the drama of the liturgy—the average illiterate peasant would be continually receiving a subliminal catechism![15]

The same was probably true in nineteenth-century industrial England. Only since the Second World War, as sociologist Grace Davie has postulated, has the general British populace had the time to travel along the Christian behaving-believing-belonging spectrum. Davie suggests that a much more radical, spiral process is occurring, so that there is no consistent believing-belonging-behaving path into the Jesus-shaped community—but somewhere along it, the challenges and questions of identity and believers' baptism occur.[16] The postwar decline in churchgoing (even church contact) means that fewer individuals have that "subliminal catechism," so their knowledge of, and conformity to, the Christian faith has to be nurtured much more fully. The

13. Schmemann, *Water and the Spirit*.

14. Duffy, *Stripping of the Altars*, 280–82.

15. Duffy, *Stripping of the Altars*, 47–52.

16. Davie, *Religion in Britain*.

question then is: what is the right point upon that journey of understanding to formalize belonging—and the sacrament(s) which accompany it?

To choose to be baptized as a believer today is a radical act. It goes against the values and flow of contemporary post-Christendom society. Being baptized does not just signify the desire and hunger to commit to Jesus-shaped values, openly eating together, and egalitarian community; it also declares a personal commitment to a new identity "in Christ." One is choosing to join an alternative, countercultural community and way of life, unto death and beyond!

"By means of its baptismal theology, Anabaptism was more consistent than other forms of Christian tradition in insisting that a sacrament is the point of intersection between grace and faith."[17] Some could argue that Orthodoxy is equally logical in administering infant baptism, then first chrismation and the Eucharist in a unified rite. We would argue that a believer's baptism is at its most sacramental when the candidate has prayerfully prepared, then professed their own belief in Christ, experienced personally the waters of baptism and the joy of being welcomed into the arms of a supportive and eucharistic Jesus-shaped community. For infants being baptized it is not at all the same experience—although, for some parents, it is undoubtedly a "moment of grace" and therefore has sacramental power. Whether the journey of pilgrimage is that of a believer experiencing full immersion, or a parent watching as the sign of the cross is made on their child's forehead, the in-breaking of God creates sacramental moments.

Eucharist

"Eucharist" is just one of many names for the bread-and-cup sharing, emanating from the accounts of Jesus and his first disciples in the Upper Room on the night before his crucifixion. In this section of the book we will use the term *Eucharist*; but we can also offer strong universal arguments for the use of *Holy Communion*, because we are sharing together with Christ and one another, within an acknowledged holy context.

The word *Eucharist* is drawn from the Greek *eucharistia*, which means "thanksgiving." It is when we are accepted for who we are before God—around the Lord's table with the others from the Jesus community, awaiting Christ's gifts of bread and wine—that we can be most truly thankful that God's in-breaking holiness is transformative. Our identity in Christ is once again bound up with this sacrament as we share bread and wine in the community of God's

---

17. John D. Rempel, in Stoffer, *Lord's Supper*, 245.

faithful people, knowing the in-breaking of holiness and grace afresh into our lives, individually and corporately. "The Communion table is the table of discipleship for all who would follow in Jesus' steps. Jesus gives us a solemn and sobering invitation: the call to follow him in life and in death."[18]

Once again the important principle of anamnesis comes into view. In the Eucharist, we are bound together with all the saints (and sinners) of God's universal church, when the in-breaking of holiness unites all God's people, from the disciples in the Upper Room to the sisters and brothers receiving bread and wine with us today, and goes forward to all gathered at the messianic banquet when God will fulfill all things. This is a radical moment, when God turns the temporal values of this earthly world upside down. We rejoice that many churches today recognize this in their liturgical prayers. For example, in the UK's former *Methodist Service Book*'s post-communion prayer, the people say together: "We thank you Lord, that you have fed us in this sacrament, united us with Christ, and given us a foretaste of the heavenly banquet, prepared for all your people."[19] Amen to that—do not let go of such theology.

Several volumes of the "After Christendom" series document different examples of one element of local eucharistic practice. They tell of different local congregations where the celebrant invites the congregation sitting "in the round" to retell the biblical narrative of the institution of the Lord's Supper in their own words, so that many contribute using material from the Gospels and the Pauline writings. In this the congregation make that narrative their own, affirming their own identity "in Christ" together at that particular table, yet acknowledging its anamnetic function: that they will be doing this "until Christ comes again in glory" (or similar words).[20] As the congregation weaves the gospel moment for themselves, they create an anticipation for the in-breaking of God's holiness.

The Eucharist does have a sociopolitical agenda, drawn from its Jewish antecedents. "Two of the distinguishing marks of the Jewish Passover are its hospitality, within the community, and the welcome to the stranger who will be fed. At the Passover table, there is bread for all."[21] We cannot gather at the eucharistic table and receive the broken bread as from Jesus' hand and then leave our sister or brother from that same circle without bread or with some other material need. John Howard Yoder, the Mennonite theologian, wrote: "Bread eaten together is economic sharing . . . that basic needs are met is a

---

18. Kreider, *Communion Shapes Character*, 135.

19. Methodist Church, *Methodist Service Book*, B17.

20. E.g., Kreider and Kreider, *Worship and Mission*, 126; Francis, *Hospitality*, 38.

21. Francis, *Hospitality*, 43.

sign of the messianic age."[22] Andrew has family experience in a number of congregations where the richer members at the Eucharist have bought homes, cars, and kitchen white goods as well as providing everyday food or clothing for their more impoverished co-congregants (Acts 2:42–47). Eucharistic hospitality and justice travel together: the reign of God cannot be the reign of God unless earthly wrongs are righted. The transformative in-breaking of God's holiness in the Eucharist has to have temporal as well as eternal significance if it is to be a sacrament.

The event described at the beginning of this chapter took place within the context of one of Britain's earliest and most prominent emerging church communities. Because it was birthed and led by an Anglican lay Church Army officer rather than an ordained Anglican priest, the weekly "bread-and-cup" moments had to be regarded as an *agape* meal or "love feast." On occasions when a full Eucharist was to be celebrated, the local parish priest attended to preside. Regardless of context, the individual and corporate identity of those involved, and the signifiers used, the fact that it was set within the Anglican tradition meant that ordained presidency was a prerequisite.

For the vast majority of the group the finer distinctions between an *agape* and theologically correct Eucharist were less relevant than the experience of the in-breaking of God in *all those* bread-and-cup moments in *that* company of God's people. Indeed for many of them, themselves fully versed in the ecclesiological traditions from which they came, it was a joy to be able to challenge and stretch them within the context of a gathering expecting to experience the transformative in-breaking of God's holy grace.

If the Eucharist is to be a sacrament, it must allow the radical act of gathering, and waiting upon God with bread and wine to burst through our preconceived expectations—including our precious theological niceties, such as whether participants need to be physically present or can do so online. The gathering, in whichever form it is accepted it may take place (according to corporate tradition and context), will be missional in enough ways to herald the reign of God, affirm our identity in the divine, and change the world. In light of the COVID-19 pandemic, there may be times when we have to swallow our pride and accept that our gatherings are valid, even if "we've never done it like that before."

---

22. Yoder, *Body Politics*, 20–21.

The Life of the Church

"The Church is the place where the new system of relationships is to be recognised and appropriated."[23] The last paragraphs of the previous section help us realize that it is the life of the church and our experience of God within it that will help us travel into the post-Christendom era—if we can but perceive it.

There can be no question that both baptism and Eucharist are established in the missionary writings of the first decades of Christian believers. They are formative in the shaping, mission, development, and growth of the pre-Christendom church. Excepting much later movements such as the Society of Friends (Quakers) or the Salvation Army, who exercise their Christian faith and ministries without a recognized sacramental life, the practices of baptism and Eucharist are virtually universal across Christendom and all the inherited denominations today. Whether they are called "ordinances," "tsaintsva," or "sacraments" is irrelevant to their universal, dominically inspired practice. For us as writer–theologians, this ubiquity set them apart in our thinking for post-Christendom ecclesiology and mission to be considered as universally sacramental.

We note the diversity in the 1970's Jesus Movement of North America, the current fresh expressions of church in English-speaking regions or the base church communities of liberation theology in South America or east Asia, particularly Korea's *minjung*[24] liberationism.[25] Yet for them all, the ongoing anamnestic celebration of baptism and Eucharist illustrates the essential and sacramental nature of their universal moments of God's in-breaking holiness. Whether denominational tradition will outweigh the sense of call to share moments of grace in each of their contexts in new ways still remains to be seen. Whatever the case, it is certain that bread will be broken and wine will be shared; and new Christians will be initiated into an ancient–future faith within these new and growing forms of post-Christendom, missional, Jesus-shaped movements.

Let us give this chapter's final word to Larson-Miller: "It is desire or longing, [as well as] the Christian response to divine actions, which moves communities and individuals forward, from a created good to an eternal good."[26] Now that is sacramental.

23. Green, *Only Connect*, 58.

24. Means "people's theology" and was the most politicized southeast Asian liberation theology, in its struggle for social democracy.

25. Pieris, *Asian Theology.*

26. Larson-Miller, *Sacramentality*, 110.

7

"Five for the Symbols at Your Door"[1]

I (Andrew) was driving home along the freeway after midnight, having been speaking at an evening conference. I was halted by the blue lights attending a serious accident. A police officer who saw my clerical collar said, "Father, we need you." Despite explaining I was not a Catholic priest, I was given a hi-vis jacket and escorted to the wreckage of a car, with my emergency kit of a communion pack and a bottle of olive oil. With the door removed, I knelt on the tarmac in leaking petrol, blood, and fire-retardant foam, and listened to the crushed driver's dying needs. He struggled to speak, confessing much, then struggled (together with me) through the one Hail Mary that I asked of him, before my short prayer of epiclesis. Then I pressed a crumb of bread into his mouth and smeared his lips with wine. He died as the attending paramedic (in the passenger seat) and I said the Lord's Prayer, while I was sealing the driver's forehead with a cross of oil. "He's at peace, your job's done, Father."

What was I as a Free Church presbyter doing there? That question and the nature of my response on that night, nearly thirty years ago, may have been the genesis of this book. There was an expectation that I as a Christian would and could do whatever was needed. The emergency service officers had no time for theological niceties but knew enough of faith that some ritual was needed, even if they had never thought about the implications.

1. "Five for the symbols at your door" is part of the common refrain of a folk song, known across the English-speaking world, often called "Green Grow the Rushes-O," also known as "The Twelve Prophets" (but having regional names such as "The Twelve Apostles," as in the American Ozarks) or the "Carol of Twelve Numbers." Unsurprisingly, it has a variety of deep theological connotations.

Already, we have made reference to the fact that the more historic inherited traditions observed and kept another five practices, which they also determined as "sacraments." We have already noted that these are anointing of the sick, confirmation, holy matrimony, holy orders, and penance or reconciliation. In the writing of this book, we have no desire to hurt, cause anger, or mock the feelings and beliefs of our friends, relatives, and colleagues from the Orthodox, Roman Catholic, and Anglo-Catholic Churches, and the autocephalic Catholic orders who both venerate and acknowledge these five historic (rather than "biblical") sacraments.

As we have undertaken our respective itinerant speaking ministries recently we have, on several occasions, asked participants at clergy study days, parish conferences, theological forums, etc., to answer a short written questionnaire about "sacraments after Christendom." Although our sample was small, the answers to questions, almost unsurprisingly, fell along the lines of the respondents' inherited traditions. Only two Roman Catholic parish conferences declared any practice beyond baptism and Eucharist to be sacraments. The only three Orthodox respondents were remarkably gracious about other communions not even having sacraments or preferring to call them "ordinances." It was from Baptist, Quaker, radical, and Anabaptist groups that there was most objection to ascribing any practice—unless it was "declaredly of the gospel"—to be a sacrament.[2] It was these comments that helped confirm our personal thinking in this chapter.

What we seek to do in this chapter is recognize the historicity of these five declared sacraments, while posing questions about the nature of the debate they create as we increasingly move into this post-Christendom landscape. This chapter's opening illustration demonstrates how issues about ministry and individual expectation, even intention, surround these five sacramental observations. Indeed they have been central to the life of those who have chosen to be of God's church, which is not the choice of a vast majority of British people and increasing numbers elsewhere in the English speaking world.

Anointing of the Sick

At the point of death the anointing of the sick is commonly known as the "last rites." Consisting of confession with consequent absolution, Eucharist, and the *viaticum* (prayers that include anointing), the purpose is to release the soul into God's hands as the body undergoes earthly death. No reader should

---

2. It was the historic Reformers who determined that coercive control and the abuses perpetrated by certain clergy and bishops should end. They also declared that only a ritual based on a direct command from Christ himself was sacramental.

underestimate what a sacred and sacramental moment this is for the dying, faithful Catholic (of whatever denomination) and their surrounding family. In Peter Harvey's *Death's Gifts*[3] we find a theology that declares that death is the ultimate healing, a moment of grace, when we become fully reconciled with God.

Two things are essential: the understood intentionality by those involved in such reconciliation and the action of the ordained priest to invoke the transformative in-breaking of God. Only *in extremis* (such as in a concentration camp or at a road accident) can a member of the laity,[4] which would include a presbyter of a Protestant communion, minister to the need of the dying person, in canonical Roman Catholic theology. This is why it is important that maturing members of each Christian community increasingly learn about what criteria their inherited tradition utilizes to declare something as an ordinance, a *mysterion, tsaintsva,* or sacrament.

There have always been people who have died alone—whether in war, the wilderness, homeless on city streets, or in comfortable homes. What do those believing Catholics understand of those souls? Did they die without the assurance of a pathway to heaven to meet their Creator God? More than 50 percent of the world's population lives in cities in this twenty-first century, but how many still die without a community of care which ensures their spiritual needs are met in their final earthly moments?

The anointing of the sick (which is often anointing of the dying) is perhaps one of the most paradoxical of all those rituals sometimes named "sacraments." Undoubtedly for those whose tradition demands it, anointing of the sick is possibly the ultimate sacramental moment. In the act of dying the subject believes themself to be literally cleansed and prepared to be welcomed home by Christ (John 14:1–4). To be ministered to in this way must be a great comfort, both to the participant and their loved ones. Indeed, the authors' experience of hospital visiting at end-of-life moments has invariably included prayers of blessing, interpreted, whichever way they are meant, as a sort of metaphorical cleansing and preparation for death.

Once again the challenge is not to declare whether a particular ritual practice is a sacrament, but to assess its efficacy as a sacramental act in the post-Christendom era. Initially it seems that a mind-set that questions both the Christian metanarrative and its manufactured superstructure (sometimes known as the church and its canonical rules) makes the anointing of the sick as a ritual nonsensical for the majority. Nor is it universally accepted as a sacrament among Christians. As knowledge and experience of Christianity wanes

3. Harvey, *Death's Gifts.*
4. From the Greek *laos* used within the Christian church to mean "all God's people."

among most people, the expectation of such a ritual being performed at the point of death also decreases. However, if contributing a prayer of confession and absolution, an anointing, and a blessing can be experienced as sacramental, regardless of whether the recipient is a practicing Catholic or not, who are we to deny its efficacy? Of all the rituals labeled by some as sacramental, this is the one that depends the most on the tradition, context, and identity of the recipient to create a covenantal moment of grace.

Confirmation

In previous chapters, we have referred to the rite of confirmation. Regrettably a few of our questionnaire respondents have written (or spoken to one of us) with some vitriol of their own experience of confirmation. It was an "empty rite, devoid of any sense of wonder," "just a rite of passage to appease my parents," and "if only the church had worked as hard at making church afterwards just as challenging and inspirational as they had made confirmation classes." Please recall that these are all people who have become committed Christians some time later in life, who were attending some occasion when they filled in a questionnaire for these writers. There will be a lot more for whom confirmation was an empty experience, who did not rediscover faith's commitment, probably losing even notional involvement in church and possibly abandoning any sense of belief.

Both authors have poor experiences of confirmation, whether our own or those of close friends or family. We have a real hesitation about pushing teenagers towards confirmation, preferring, if they feel it right, to wait until they can realistically understand what professing "Jesus is Lord" might mean in the world of work, long-term relationships, parenting, health crises, and bereavements. However, our preference would be to focus upon adults, who have begun making their life choices, for whom the call to discipleship is clearly recognized as countercultural, demanding rites, if not sacraments that speak into "their world."

When a candidate's faith is presented before others, within the context of their home faith community, the covenant God to whom they are committing is present. For that person, if not for everyone there, heaven is opened and a moment of grace takes place. This is why Janet can say with confidence that her best confirmation candidate was a thirteen-year-old, who displayed a maturity of faith rarely seen at that age. His confirmation was an occasion none of those present would ever forget—and he had become an ordained URC elder by the age of eighteen.

The intentionality of declaring personal discipleship is essential if confirmation is to have any meaning. Is it appropriate to say that something is sacramental if the intention and transformation is only that from God rather than the human recipient? What are we saying about the church if we accept such thinking? A key issue within the debate is: who are the sacraments for? And what motivation needs to be behind them if they are to be defined as "moments of grace"? We have already described our experience of being approached by parents wishing to have their infant christened without any particular faith motivation. The same is surely to be said for confirmation, and indeed any other moment of grace. For it to be sacramental there has to be a relational aspect: between God and a human being. That is surely the meaning of covenant: that God steps in as a response to human faith.

There is a major question of Christian initiation to be addressed, both by churches who institute it and those who put forward candidates for it—whether through baptism or confirmation—for tradition and habit are not necessarily the same thing. Simply baptizing or confirming someone because "that's what you do" is no longer an appropriate response to a request for either. The call on God's people is to embody Christ's words, works, and ways in and for every generation. As Christendom fades into a new era, the question must be asked about whether new creative ways are needed to enable sacramental moments that fulfill the need for those professing Christ to be initiated into a noticeably adult part of their faith journey. It is not our task to tell churches to ditch their traditions—rather, to challenge their meaning and efficacy as a missional church after Christendom.

Holy Matrimony

What is holy matrimony? At what point can marriage be classed as a sacrament? How can a member of another faith or an atheist have a marriage which can be declared a Christian sacrament if they have no intention for God-in-Christ to be transformative within it? How many tourists using Sunset Strip wedding chapels view their wedding to be Christian or intend their marriage to be lifelong? There can hardly be a reader of this book who has not witnessed an abusive marriage from their workplace, in their home neighborhood, or perhaps even in their own wider family. It is not just social scientists who rightly question whether in such circumstances a wedding ceremony could be described as sacramental and if there can be a universal concept called "Christian marriage."

We have already explained that marriage was once taught to be an indissoluble sacrament in order to maintain the stability of society and keep clear understandings of family lines and inheritance. At that time marriages could be conducted only within the church. The world has changed and few now truly believe that the church has such authority over their lives.

Jack Dominian, the renowned Roman Catholic marital therapist, posits the view that for a marriage to be Christian, it must not only be contracted and the personal vows exchanged within the couple's worshipping community, but it must be sustained by *both* partners' lifelong involvement in that Christian community's life for it to be continually nurtured and transformed by the grace of God.[5] Contemporary Christian theology faces many challenges concerning marriage,[6] civil partnerships,[7] and divorce within the Christian community.[8]

Perhaps what is most radical in today's Western world of serial monogamy are those couples who take on the vows of marriage creatively, enabling their relationship to be a lifelong union: "'Til death do us part." Their committed life together may be worthy of the description of sacrament, but is the Christian community using that word to mean the moment of their exchange of vows, or the transformative family celebration of the wedding day, or the whole of their life together? If the church demands that it is all of those "moments in time" for it to be sacramental, we have to ask how its constituent local churches cope with both their teaching and missiology, as well as those in their midst whose marriages fall apart, without consigning them to the second-hand bucket.

For the purposes of this book, it is worth reiterating the question about how long the sacrament of marriage is supposed to last. Does the Holy Spirit act at the moment the vows are taken and the marriage blessed? And is the result to unite the couple in a state of permanent grace? A pragmatic response might be to say that no two people can live in a state of perpetual sacrament. However, that is not to say that the commitment made on both sides is not faith-filled, nor that the Holy Spirit is unable to make a union holy. For those who are getting married as Christians, before their family and friends and within the context of their Christian community, undoubtedly the moment of their marriage blessing is sacramental—for their belief is that the covenantal vows they make to each other are symbolic of their covenant relationship with God.

Once again there is a paradox at work. In the post-Christendom era, marriage is a ritual, but is it always sacramental in nature?

5. Dominian, *Marriage, Faith and Love*, 230–54.
6. Durber, ed., *Man and Woman Made*.
7. Wilson, *More Perfect Union?*
8. Nichols, *Ending Marriage*.

Holy Orders

Christian history books tell us that, during the first centuries of Christianity, there were many bogus but allegedly Christian communities; therefore it was important that the orthodoxy of leaders to Jesus and the Spirit could be affirmed. One simple test was who had commissioned them: being able to show that they had been "set apart" for a particular ministry, by a chain of known and recognized leaders back to the post-Pentecost disciples, was important.[9] This was a basic form of "apostolic succession" to safeguard orthodoxy and leadership. Much later it became stylized[10]—almost like biblical genealogies— but was vital among autocephalic[11] traditions to demonstrate the orthodox succession of priesthood.[12]

The Pauline-based apostolic writings offer us at least two patterns of ministry. One is a hierarchical order of bishops, priests, and deacons (1 Tim 5:17–22)—with military echoes of Roman officers, centurions, and foot-soldiers—who *seem* to be set apart from the general people of God. The other pattern is one rooted more in the nature of spiritual gifts (Gk.: *charismata*) when people are empowered—"Some are called to be . . ." (see Eph 4:11)— within a more egalitarian team-approach of mutually cooperating ministries. The latter was never going to fit easily into either a need for "apostolic succession" or a one-size-fits-all approach to ministry or priesthood. Paul's acceptance of a variety of practices and his commissioning of women (e.g., Phoebe) with important tasks[13] lead us to question those who declare the rigidity of his position.

One can easily imagine how, in later centuries, such rigidity led to a restrictive process, where individuals could be commissioned for ministries only by certain of their predecessors. Equally, it becomes logical in maintaining a singular defining pattern of bishops, priests, and deacons to understand how orthodoxy and (holy) orders of ministry became controlling principles. Until the great East-West schism of 1054 CE, priests were often married and still have to be today within the Orthodox Communion. Within the Western Roman-based church, celibacy was imposed to enable priests to be subject to

---

9. Rausch, *Towards a Truly Catholic Church*, 144–45.

10. Think "ordained by" instead of "begat" in a recurring list.

11. These are self-headed groups, often from the broader catholic traditions, who do not recognize the authority of the pope or one of the historic patriarchs.

12. Armstrong, *Order of Dionysis*, 120–21.

13. McKnight, *Reading Romans Backwards*.

movement by the bishop (hence "holy orders") and enable conformity, if not uniformity, of working disciplines, lifestyle, and practice.[14]

During the past forty years, a broader debate has been developing as ministry lessons from the South American base ecclesial communities, the Anglican Communion's differences about the ordination of women, helpful books,[15] and the European emerging churches' landscape have grown. While at ecumenical seminary, Andrew was responsible (with senior ordinands from other traditions) for organizing a semester-long study of different theologies of ministry, using college faculty and local clergy as educators, discussion facilitators, and resource persons. Three different theologies of ministry were recognized then, and it is fair to suggest that even more are now emerging as ecclesial communities respond to the ministerial needs within their contexts:

- *Sacramental*—affirming the nature of priesthood, as an ontological change within ordination to that role. The staunchest defenders of ordination as sacrament are from a Catholic tradition.

- *Charismatic*—those radical or predominantly emerging churches which recognize the roles and gifting of particular individuals and commission them to those particular roles, such as worship leader (a cantor–musician role) in the Hillsong movement.

- *Functional*—a predominantly Free Church understanding of commissioning (although they might call it "ordination") to a role such as pastor or "minister of word and sacrament," yet the equipping for that role may either have been college-based or training in another congregation.

No longer is there a single theology of ministry but instead a rich variety of understandings.[16] There are opposing views, some pejorative, about the words "priest" or "priestcraft" (meaning the administration of the sacraments). Whether those exercising these different forms of leadership are described as priests, pastors, ministers, or presbyters is less relevant than recognizing that all are an appropriate means of facilitating different yet shared understandings of ordained or commissioned ministry.

Holy orders, or ordination, is one of the two Roman Catholic sacraments known as "sacraments of service," of which one is understood to result in an ontological transformation: essentially, the person is changed for all time from a normal layperson into a priest. There is a stark opposition between this understanding of ordination and that of the Free Church traditions, who ordain

---

14. Thurian, *Priesthood and Ministry*.

15. E.g., Moore, ed., *Man, Woman and Priesthood*.

16. Anderson, ed., *Theological Foundations*.

an individual to a certain role at a certain time and place in history. While there is certainly a recognition within their community, it is clear that there is no precedent in tradition, context, or identity to warrant Free Church ordination as a sacrament, or that all commissioned ministry is sacramental. Even if someone is set apart with the biblical practice of "prayer and the laying on of hands," it does not necessarily imply that they have accepted this as either ordination or a sacrament.[17]

Penance[18] and Reconciliation

Much Roman Catholic humor is built around sacramental disciplines, such as going to Mass or the nature of penance following confession. It points to the absurdity of the extreme demands once made by priests of the faithful congregants to undertake non-fruitful acts such as penance. One of the most radical Catholics of the last century was Dorothy Day, the cofounder (with Peter Maurin) of the pacifist, goods-sharing, servant Catholic Worker movement, with its newspaper and cooperative households. She wrote: "Penance seems to be ruled out today . . . It is a penance to work, to give oneself to others."[19] Hers was the penance of serving others to her very last possession, and not some liturgical repetition or the discomfort of a hair shirt.

The primary intention of penance is to help remind ourselves of the need to be "put right" with God. It is intended to heal the brokenness caused by the sin of the believer. The former Benedictine monk Peter Harvey summarized his life's creative teaching in his book, *Death's Gifts*: death is the ultimate healing, when we become fully reconciled with God.[20] This is the fullest human-divine encounter and affirms our eternal identity "in Christ." Likewise, Martin Israel—a senior lecturer at the Royal College of Surgeons, UK, and an Anglican parish priest—taught that healing is a sacrament. But Israel was referring to the spiritual reconciliation with the physiological ailment.[21] Illness and injury are not human sins requiring some expiation through confession and penance (although they may be caused by the willful sins of others, be that personal or industrial). Neither death nor spiritual reconciliation are sacraments, because the ending of our mortal life puts us beyond the reach

17. Beasley-Murray, ed., *Anyone for Ordination*.

18. Anciaux, *Penance*.

19. Day, *Little By Little*, 179–80.

20. Harvey, *Death's Gifts*.

21. Israel, *Healing as Sacrament*.

of the church and its teaching, while illness or injury are part of life's natural journey, requiring no expiation.

While we believe the Roman Catholic Communion has the absolute right to declare the nature of penance in their tradition as a sacrament, we recognize that the post-Christendom world will find far more empathy with the liberation theology's base church communities and Catholic Worker members, who will question the "Ten Hail Marys" style of penance, preferring the notion of penance through service to others. However, the fact that such "servant-penances" are being advocated by *some* Roman Catholic priests indicates a changing understanding of both absolution and penance. A priest in Manchester tells the story of a parishioner who came to confess her negative thoughts about a neighbor. "Bake a cake and take it round to her," he said to her from behind the confessional curtain. "Apologize to her and ask her forgiveness."

We have witnessed some of the truly creative, contemporary, corporate rites of mutual confession, as practiced by some Lutheran and Reformed denominations, in which both presbyter and people make alternate professions of confession and contrition. The Taizé Community also have adopted this prophetic pattern of mutual confession both within their order and in some of their public liturgies.[22] Their consequent communal response in true service to others invites the recognition of the in-breaking of God's holiness, because in that human-divine encounter, a true moment of grace is achieved, facilitating the mutual lifting of whatever guilt. Whether or not it is labeled "sacrament," this is surely a "sacramental moment."

"Five for the Symbols at Your Door"

Opposite the big hospital in one of northern England's largest cities, I (Andrew) got to know well the Catholic priests whose church and presbytery faced the hospital's main gate. Their weekly Saturday lunchtime "Mass for the Sick" and midweek "Healing Service with Anointing" attracted a stream of patients, often pushed in wheelchairs by relatives. The integrity of their ministry and their belief in their seven sacraments was almost palpable. For them, the dwelling of God among them in community was both mediated and recognized in their sacramental acts. As Lizette Larson-Miller writes: "Sacramentality is about encounter between the living God and God's living people. If we return to the theological understanding of God dwelling among us and within

---

22. Thurian, *Confession.*

us, then the dwelling of the Church, the Body of Christ, whether temporary or long-term is a crucial dimension."[23]

What our communion or community of congregations believes, whether at global or city level, to be sacramental or is a sacrament is vital to the way we offer ministry from our doors. Those Catholic priests exercise their ministries just as much as do Anglicans and Episcopalians, who declare there are only the two Christ-centered sacraments of the gospel—baptism and Eucharist—or some of our Anabaptist friends who reject the concept of sacraments altogether, favoring the word *ordinance*. As Brother Alois, Prior of Taizé, often says: "The truth of God cannot be contained in any one church"—and he was raised as a faithful Roman Catholic.

This chapter has reflected upon five of the declared sacraments which are shared across the broader catholic traditions. They act as "symbols at the door," safeguarding catholic church disciplines, and as "pillars of faith" for the encouragement and building up of individual belief. Within their traditions and contexts these sacred activities both mediate and demonstrate God's covenant love dwelling within their communities. It is a key part of their identity as Christian community, whether or not other Christian traditions choose to recognize them as such. That the Protestant traditions, as well as the various "historic radical" and "emerging church" communities, have chosen not to adopt them as sacraments does not make them less vital to those who have. It is simply that, across the breadth of Christian tradition, different communities have determined the number and nature of sacraments to reflect their evolving contexts, traditions, theological understandings, and sense of identity as ecclesial bodies. Once this is acknowledged and recognized, it is easy to treat these differing traditions with equal levels of respect and mutuality.

"A Touch Too Much"

How can anointing not involve contact when it requires human touch and the oils of unction to impart the strength of God to others in weakness? The efficacy of confirmation requires the presiding minister to lay hands upon each candidate while praying for them. How often have you witnessed marriages when the celebrant has not joined the couple's hands together or there has been no "giving and receiving of rings"? When appointed leaders are ordained, authorized or commissioned, they are usually "set apart" by the biblical practice of others gathering around to "pray and to share in the laying on of hands." Penance can be channeled into cerebral spiritual exercises, but how

---

23. Larson-Miller, *Sacramentality*, 170.

often can reconciliation not involve a handshake, a hug, or service between wronged parties?

The COVID-19 pandemic has further challenged the church in its theology, practice, and rubrics of the five historic sacraments, not just in catholic circles but for those who have accepted them as practices or ordinances or simply adopted them more locally and informally in radical movements. All require both human proximity and some form of human touch for them to be properly shared; enforced social distancing destroys their very nature. How much will the 2020 pandemic draw some in to the "community of the safeguarded touch" or alienate others? To put this in perspective, think how many folk in pre-COVID-19 (often inherited) congregations shied away from the "sharing of the Peace" as it was "a touch too much," as one United Reformed Church elder and her Anglican husband described it. Sacraments involve unmasked human contact; we say more about this in the next chapter.

This chapter has also raised important questions that we will take into the remaining chapters of the book. Who are the sacraments for? What motivation needs to be behind them if they are to be defined as "moments of grace"? Do sacraments have to be recognized universally, or is it okay that some traditions have none, two, or seven? Most importantly of all, this chapter has prompted the question of what exactly happens at that sacramental moment; and to what extent identity, context, tradition, and covenant are influencing factors on what participants believe is happening, both at that moment and afterwards

At a seminary that generally taught there are only two sacraments (baptism and Holy Communion), Andrew learned from experienced presybyters the value of keeping a small bottle of olive oil and a ready-charged communion kit, as well as about the rich spirituality of other traditions. That night on the freeway, he thanked God that he had.

8

Anointing

In 1998 a man with whom I (Janet) played on a darts team was rushed to hospital. The diagnosis was serious: meningitis and tuberculosis contracted as a consequence of HIV/AIDS. Over the next few months I visited him regularly. He was a lapsed Catholic, but a friend of his had given him some holy water and he developed a habit of dabbing some on, hoping to invoke some sort of divine intervention in his recovery. Shortly afterwards I went to the Holy Land. He asked me to bring back more holy water. I filled a bottle with tap water from my hotel and brought it back, decanting some into his "holy water" vial before going to visit him.

I will never forget the moment I scattered the water and made the sign of the cross on his head and hands. We weren't in church, I wasn't ordained, and the water definitely wasn't "holy"—but at that moment Christ became present for both of us. My friend's face shone and tears fell down his cheeks. In his eyes he knew he was forgiven, loved, and free. From the church's perspective there was absolutely nothing in that act that qualified it to be a sacrament. And yet . . .

Anointing with Oil

It might seem that, in writing a full chapter on "anointing," the authors wish to rehash an argument already made in the previous chapter. This is not so. While "anointing of the sick," or "extreme unction" as it was once called, is considered one of the seven sacraments in some Christian traditions, this is certainly not the only—or even most prominent—reason for using oil to anoint believers historically. This chapter is therefore included to trace the origins, history, and purposes of anointing as a Christian ritual; then to assess the extent to which these forms of anointing might be considered a "sacrament" or "sacramental" practice.

Anointing in Historical and Biblical Context

Anointing is the practice of taking oil, water, balm (oil mixed with balsam), or another substance, and scattering or rubbing it on a person's body. As a ritual act it is usually carried out for one or more of three purposes:

- To invoke healing or power;
- To convey blessing or forgiveness; and
- To confirm membership or identity of an individual within a particular religious context.

It is not confined to any one religion, indeed there are records of anointing being practiced, with a variety of spiritual purposes, among cultures as varied the Ancient Egyptian, Persian Zoroastrian, and indigenous Aboriginal peoples. It is recorded in the Hebrew Scriptures as playing a key role in ancient Jewish religion to identify something as sacred or someone as holy. When Moses sets up the tabernacle place of meeting, God commands him thus:

> You shall take the anointing-oil, and anoint the tabernacle and all that is in it, and consecrate it and all its furniture, so that it shall become holy. You shall also anoint the altar of burnt-offering and all its utensils, and consecrate the altar, so that the altar shall be most holy. You shall also anoint the basin with its stand, and consecrate it. Then you shall bring Aaron and his sons to the entrance of the tent of meeting, and shall wash them with water, and put on Aaron the sacred vestments, and you shall anoint him and consecrate him, so that he may serve me as priest. You shall bring his sons also and put tunics on them, and anoint them, as you anointed their father, that they may serve me as priests: and their anointing shall admit them to a perpetual priesthood throughout all generations to come. (Exod 40:9–15)

In the Hebrew Scriptures ritual anointing is nearly always accompanied by the making of sacrificial offerings; an act which, as we have already seen, was understood as a moment of grace, enabling God to step into the mundanity of the world and intervene.

Jesus himself is not recorded as anointing anyone with oil. Of course this does not mean he did not do it, but if anointing is understood to be an act symbolizing the presence of God, having God incarnate present in the form of Jesus Christ removes any need for anointing. Indeed, the term "Messiah" means "anointed one," and Jesus' laying on of hands would have been enough. By contrast, the disciples are sent out practicing anointing in Jesus' name (Mark 6:13).

As we have already noted, the issues arising from sacramental practices during the COVID-19 pandemic demonstrate how Jesus' own practice of touch within ministry provides the model for his followers, then and now. In chapter 2, we saw that Jesus' incarnation and his use of touch was not just "intimate and earthy" but also essential to human-divine encounters.

In his second letter to the Corinthians, Paul encourages the members of the church in their new identity as Christians by telling them that "it is God who establishes us with you in Christ and has anointed us, by putting his seal on us and giving us his Spirit in our hearts as a first installment" (2 Cor 1:21–22). The author of Hebrews advises the Jewish converts that they are made holy by how they express their faith: "You have loved righteousness and hated wickedness; therefore God, your God, has anointed you with the oil of gladness beyond your companions" (Heb 1:9).

John, in his first letter, explains that the consequence of Christ's anointing "teaches [them] about all things, and is true and is not a lie" (1 John 2:20, 27). A text often referred to in association with anointing of the sick as a sacrament is James 5:14: "Are any among you sick? They should call for the elders of the church and have them pray over them, anointing them with oil in the name of the Lord."

It is clear, then, that in the New Testament apostolic writings, there are two forms of anointing: first, that which has been bestowed by God as a blessing, in recognition of the recipient's new identity as a Christian. The second is related to the healing of the sick.

Two Types of Anointing in the Early Church

We know that, by the beginning of the third century, two types of anointing were commonplace in the church. Everett Ferguson describes one as "anointing the five senses of the body with oil consecrated by a bishop, laying on of hands, and prayer for the healing of the body and forgiveness of sins."[1] However, it is clear from what the bishop and theologian Hippolytus (ca. 170–235 CE) writes that, as well as an anointing oil for "exorcism," there was also another for "thanksgiving." Not only did the early Christians imbibe sanctified oil of thanksgiving as part of their communal meals, but also both

---

1. Ferguson, "Sacraments," 137.

types were incorporated into their baptism ceremony. The oil of exorcism was used to symbolize the forgiveness of sins and reception of the Holy Spirit, and the thanksgiving oil to signify the recipient's new identity as a member of the Christian community.[2]

This form of anointing was similarly used at confirmation, or chrismation as it is also known. Rather than being a sacrament in its own right, anointing was a vital ritual activity incorporated into a sacramental act, used in a very similar way to foot washing as an ordinance in some Christian traditions on Maundy Thursday. This seems a logical consequence of being a Jesus-believing movement with a large proportion of members directly descended from Jews. In a tradition descended from Moses, it was through the act of anointing that those present were "made holy." During the sacramental acts of baptism, confirmation, and Eucharist—the three sacraments still identified as the most important in the Eastern tradition[3]—those participating were "made holy" by virtue of their identity "in Christ."

Anointing and the Christendom Church

The history of how the sacraments developed in the Christian church is well rehearsed elsewhere in this book. Suffice to say, it was during the eighth century—as East met West, Christianity encountered Islam, and the struggle for intellectual and land rights took hold—that anointing itself became utilized sacramentally by the church in the West. Its purpose was ostensibly to convey blessing or forgiveness, or to invoke healing. In reality its purpose, in a time when corporate cultural identities were in flux, was to consolidate the individual identities of those who were Christian—either spiritually or culturally—and to give them confidence that, as the chosen children of God, salvation and the promise of eternal life that went with it was assured. Meanwhile the Eastern Orthodox Church continued to utilize a much looser definition of sacrament: "a holy thing that brings together and unites in itself two aspects—the material/visible/human and the spiritual/invisible/divine." Just as veneration of the cross and the use of icons were considered "sacramental," so too was the preparation and blessing of the chrism (oil mixed with balsam) by a bishop.[4]

By the time of the Reformation controversy, with its furious exchanges about what constituted a sacrament, anointing had been split into two types:

2. Cuming, ed., *Hippolytus*, 6–10, 19–20.
3. Avvakumov, "Sacramental Ritual."
4. Avvakumov, "Sacramental Ritual," 254.

unctio extrema, to do with penance, and *unctio infirmorum*, to do with heal-ing.[5] However, it wasn't that simple, as *unctio extrema*—the ritual that pre-pared someone for the afterlife—was considered sacramental, while *unctio infirmorum*—which symbolized the need for healing—was not. As we stated in the previous chapter: the Reformers, determined that coercive control and the abuses perpetrated by certain clergy and bishops should end, declared that any ritual based not on a direct command from Christ himself was not in itself sacramental.

Meanwhile in the East, the focus on redemption from sin was also prominent in the mind of Orthodox theologians such as Metrophanes Crito-poulos (ca. 1589–1639), who considered the Christian life as being marked by the trinity of: reconciliation with the Father; incorporation into Christ's body through Holy Communion; and, the life of the Spirit in the soul, symbolized by *unctio infirmorum*. This "sacramental triad" is punctuated by the use of anointing, as are the other sacraments, particularly *unctio extrema*.[6] In the United States sacramental practice mirrored the traditions from which the migrants hailed. Anointing accompanied baptism and confirmation/chrisma-tion, as well as being administered to the sick and dying. However, anointing with "oil of thanksgiving" is rarely referred to as a common contemporary Christian practice on either side of the Atlantic.

It was at the Council of Florence in 1439 that the Western church de-clared that anointing "shall not be given to any except the sick who are in fear of death," and it wasn't until 1972 that the subject was revisited by the Vatican. The term "in fear of death" was changed to "dangerously ill," but still there was no revisitation of the idea that anointing, as a sacramental activity, be anything other than for forgiveness or healing as a redemptory process during times of crisis.[7] Certainly in his recent book, *Why Sacraments?*, Andrew Davison, writ-ing from an Anglo-Catholic perspective, makes no allusion to the existence of, or need for, anointing with oil of thanksgiving. For him the sacrament of anointing is about achieving the salvation instituted through baptism and maintained through confirmation and eucharistic practice.[8] From an Episco-pal perspective, Lizette Larson-Miller's examination of sacramentality focuses on the paschal mystery and real presence, rather than exploring rituals that might stretch her sacramental theology beyond baptism and the Eucharist. The many contributors to the *Oxford Handbook of Sacramental Theology*, consisting of nearly seven hundred pages, make virtually no reference to

5. Walters, *Notes on the Sign*, 324.

6. Butcher, "Orthodox Sacramental Theology," 334.

7. Davison, *Why Sacraments?*, 120.

8. Davison, *Why Sacraments?*, 120–21.

unemployed craftsmen and trainee Church of Scotland ministers as members. Together they forged a common life, rebuilding the ruined Benedictine abbey on the remote isle of Iona, creating an agreed daily prayer life and commitment to peacemaking, charitable giving, and justice-and-peace activism, upon return to their self-supporting livelihoods and homes.[12] Now that the members are spread across most of the world, they continue those same commitments and professions of faith, meeting as a plenary community for a week residentially at least annually.

This pattern of network or dispersed community has found a growing appeal in the last generation, often nurtured by Celtic spirituality. In the UK, groups such as the Ashram Community (originally from Sheffield), the Community of Aidan and Hilda, and the Northumbria Community have all developed vital publishing enterprises, offering both high-quality daily liturgy (for home and individual use) and advocacy of this mode of sharing Jesus-shaped vision. Experience of their life together, during their residential plenary gatherings, often draws the comment of it being sacramental. In North America, the work of the Reba Place Fellowship near Evanston, Illinois,[13] with its communal households, dynamic congregations, and over sixty years of history is exemplary among the thirty or so similar communities listed on our current database for that continent.

In over ninety countries, the work of the *Chemin Neuf* (Fr.: new way) network community, with its retreats, Ignatian teaching programmes, and marriage enrichment courses, is avowedly Roman Catholic but has members from other traditions, too. Most network communities seek to be multidenominational across their membership.

Communal Households

Among others, the Ashram, the Bruderhof, Catholic Worker, the Mennonite and SCM movements have all used communal households successfully, as part of "developing community," as beacons of prayer, resource-sharing, study, and service or outreach. For some of their residents, such communal life has replaced churchgoing as their corporate discipleship.

The English Catholic writer and artist Eric Gill said: "I am sure that all attempts to create cells of the good life in the form of small communities are not only much to be encouraged but are the only hope."[14] Communal households,

12. MacLeod, ed., *Rebuilding*.
13. Janzen, ed., *Fire, Salt and Peace*, 128–33.
14. Ellsberg, ed., *Little by Little*, 223.

often led by a couple but not always, are such attempts. They may also be short-term (e.g., during undergraduate years) or for a longer-term purpose.[15] Dorothy Day, the cofounder of Catholic Worker communal households, commented about needing "to endure the pinpricks of community living."[16] However, sometimes those pinpricks can become holes which can undermine any sacramental activity.

The positive Yellow Doors Community's story, as a series of four linked communal Christian households in east Hull, England, has been told elsewhere.[17] Sadly, since then its demise has become known in a marital break-up, the premature death of another householder, and the enforced work transfer of a third homeowner. These crippling blows felled that community, its local witness, and service to so many in the neighborhood.

This was as nothing to the recent, nationally publicized downfall of the UK's Jesus Army, with its large number of linked, highly disciplined communal households, organized mission strategy, and large gathered congregations. Internet searches will reveal allegations of abuse of vulnerable adults, violence, and sexual abuse, causing the trustees and leadership teams to disperse the households and dissolve the organization.

Even more recently, the allegations of abuse made by several of his female coworkers against the late Jean Vanier—the founder of the international L'Arche Community with its many communal households that include very vulnerable people—has raised again questions of the accountability of leaders and the need for plural integrity within communities.

While Yellow Doors became victim to various ordinary human happenings, it appears that the Jesus Army or Vanier allegations may prove to be far more sinister. Would you have wanted these communities to be decreed to be a sacrament?

New Monasticism

Since the year 2000, there has been much talk, several books, and increasingly numerous examples of what is termed "new monasticism." This attempts to draw from historic monasticism both a pattern of simplifying one's lifestyle and creating a "rhythm of life"; the latter is particularly prayer-focused in the use of either daily offices or another framework for prayer. It can often seem to be a hybrid between communal households for some and a more silent,

15. Lockley, *Christian Communes*, 54–64.

16. Day, *Little By Little*, 180.

17. Francis, *Hospitality*, 65.

hermit-like existence for individuals; critics point to its introvertedness and lack of accountability. However, at its best, such as in "The Simple Way," a contemporary community in Philadelphia,[18] which also exercises servant ministries in its neighborhood, there is much to commend it.

Is "Community" a Sacrament?

It would be easy to allow this book simply to use emotions or positive and negative experiences to determine our perception as theologians and writers about whether a particular Christian practice is a sacrament. That would be subjective. We believe that we need the criteria delineated in chapter 5 to provide a more objective judgment. This is important when considering both a subject such as community and the mixed experience that its practice has engendered evidentially.

First, it is clear that community is an activity, enacted by individuals with a shared identity. If a mark of Christian community is that people join it by choice and not coercion (which is symptomatic of cults), it is an active or conscious participation rather than a passive experience. Post-Christendom is about choosing the nature, style, and experience of personal and corporate Christian identity; it is not about knowledge and doctrine so much. Therefore to join any community that has vows, limitations on personal choice, and an obligatory daily discipline requires each participating individual's active assent. One could wonder if this is why, in today's world, the number of vocations to historic forms of monastic community is falling.

Second, Christian community can be exacted only within the context of a faith community.

Third, Christian community requires personal piety and spirituality. While the whole purpose of a monastic house may be one of permanent communality and daily corporate prayer, the pattern of network or dispersed communities, communal households, and new monastic communities often involves a self-supporting life in the world—akin to that of any Sunday churchgoer. But is its principal aim to invoke a greater awareness of God in the member, the community itself, or the external observer? Hopefully it is in all three but it may be harder to persuade the member engaged in a mundane task that they are doing this to enter into the covenant presence of God. Our response is that, for the committed, confessed, and professed member who wants to follow after the words, works, and ways of Jesus, even the mundane draws us further into the covenant presence of God.

18. Claiborne, *Irresistible Revolution*.

Fourth, we might have a harder task persuading the brother in his mundane task or the sister taking a long arduous journey home after the "highs" of a dispersed community weekend that their purpose in that moment is to convey a particular spiritual idea or experience, in line with their tradition. Two things arise:

- Being able to communicate the vision, a renewed personal sense of identity, and what sacramental moment of God was shared when others were present and participating; and,

- Understanding how one relates to the traditions from which that community has gained a distinctive life.

Fifth, recognizing Christian community as an entity causes any observer to notice the diversity of practice, symbols, and signifiers. There is little in common between an activist communal household ministering to east Birmingham's urban poor, being a long-term retreatant at the rural Benedictine Worth Abbey in Sussex, and an Iona Community member's experience at their annual residential week except common meals, daily prayer, and a sense of belonging to a wider whole in the name of Jesus. There may also be similar but different sacramental moments. The different liturgies, words, and symbols used in those three experiences mean that there is not an agreed set of specific practices to make community a sacrament.

Perhaps those writing in favor of post-Christendom perspectives have to recognize the wisdom of the Christendom church in not calling "community" a sacrament.

In Conclusion

We both have significant experience of Christian communities. Andrew was brought up in a seminary where a parent taught, while Janet lived for a time as a volunteer at a Christian conference center in a Swiss chateau. We were both live-in members of our own seminary communities, we have both been retreatants, guests, and visiting teachers in residential and dispersed communities, and Andrew has experienced living in or leading three different communal households. At present, we both live in our own nuclear family households, yet we retain respect for many forms of community, whether monastic or dispersed.

However, we perceive that within post-Christendom, the role of self-supporting network (or dispersed) communities—who live "in the world" separately but following the same daily discipline of prayer and activism—will have an increasing influence as well as small communal (possibly common-purse) activist households, e.g., Catholic Worker houses or the former London Mennonite Centre.

Sacramental moments often present themselves within the context of community gatherings, whether as part of a lifetime-professed order or in a coming together of a dispersed community. Our experience of the Ashram, Bruderhof, Catholic Worker, Iona, Northumbria, and Taizé Communities as well as retreats in several historic monastic abbeys is that these communities rejoice in the sacramental nature of life within their respective contexts but none expects their community to be a sacrament.

Simplicity enables us to live intensely, without the fetters of stifling wealth or the burden of increasing acquisition of material things. That simplicity of lifestyle and spirituality can make anyone, whatever the nature of their community, become open to the sacramental moments of the in-breaking of God.

10

Foot Washing

Before I (Andrew) began formal duties as a hospice chaplain, I had my hands washed thoroughly by the senior nurse—it took over five minutes. Before my next shift, the hospice director washed my hands similarly again before asking me to wash the hands of that same senior nurse. It was a humbling experience. The nurse then told me that this part of everyone's induction program was to remind us all that we are each serving everyone's needs in this "place of dying and celebrating life" (what a powerful way to express the ministry of a hospice), while also learning to wash one's hands properly for sound medical reasons. It was not just humbling, it was intimate, earthy, natural, and involved human touch.

"Three rituals closely associated with early Christian churches' practice of the Lord's Supper are the bread-and-cup ceremony, the foot-washing service and the kiss of peace."[1] This quote is from the Mennonite liturgist and musician Eleanor Kreider, whose own tradition is among the leading proponents of foot washing in worship. Kreider reminds us that those three rituals are intimate, involving touch—factors that we noted in chapter 5 were often symbolic of sacramental action.

Foot washing *can* be a sacramental action, depending upon its context. In the earliest days of the Christian church, it was often part of the ministry of widows (1 Tim. 5:10), who washed the feet of prisoners and other confined persons, such as the sick or those in need. This practice was not communal but private; it did not take place within public worship and had all but expired by the coming of Christendom in the fourth century. Foot washing was a practice commented on by several church fathers—such as Augustine, Cassian, John

1. Kreider, *Communion*, 158.

Chrysostom, and Athanasius, all revered leaders and theologians in the second to fourth centuries.[2] By the time of the fourth-century St. Ambrose, foot washing became much more associated with Christian initiation; this pattern developed during the expansion of Western monasticism. The existence of a *pedilavium* or footbath in most medieval monastic buildings points to the potential ubiquity of the practice.[3]

The practice of foot washing enabled a ministry of human touch and care, particularly to those who might be otherwise denied it, such as prisoners and monks. The practice was clearly rooted in Jesus' own ministry but as Eleanor Kreider further explains: "John 13, with no mention of the bread-and-cup ceremony, but portraying Jesus' act of washing his disciples' feet . . . thereby emphasizes Jesus' command to his followers to imitate his act, serving one another in humility and love."[4]

The John 13 passage sets a pattern of service forward for the Christian community. Jesus declares: "I give you a new commandment, that you love one another. Just as I have loved you, you also should love one another." This "new commandment," or *novum mandatum* in the Latin Bible, sets forward the pattern of service that is still with us today. It is from the Latin tag *mandatum* that the word "Maundy" is derived; hence we have Maundy Thursday in Holy Week, when the John 13 narrative is most often recalled and ritually reenacted in the Western church.

Learning from Our Past and Present

Within the pre-Christendom Church, one of the later church fathers, Ambrose of Milan, describes foot washing. It took place during public worship in Holy Week, when the bishop would wash the feet of choirboys. The theology involved assumes this is the greater ministering to the lesser, echoing Jesus and the disciples, but what this says about a hierarchical church is for brief comment later and expansion in another book. Are we not servants of one another in the name of Christ? Equally from that period of the early church, archaeologists have discovered small troughs (or *pedilavia*), next to baptisteries, which it is assumed were used for washing the feet of the newly baptized, as a (theological) symbol of mutual service.[5]

2. Thomas, *Footwashing.*

3. McGowan, "Missing Sacrament?"

4. Kreider, *Communion,* 137.

5. Whitaker, "Milan."

In the early days of sixteenth-century Dutch Anabaptism, one of its persecuted leaders, Dirk Phillips, taught that "speaking to the unconverted" was the first ordinance; baptism and sharing the bread and cup were the second ordinance; and mutual foot washing was the third ordinance.[6] For the first Anabaptists, foot washing was that important: mutuality in service *and* foot washing were an everyday part of "following after" [Ger.: *nachfolge*] the words, works, and ways of Jesus, thus becoming a vital part of their Christian witness. Phillips was succeeded in his leadership of these Dutch Anabaptists by Menno Simons, whose name was taken by the movement still active today—Mennonites.[7]

Eleanor Kreider writes movingly of her own lifelong experience as part of that foot-washing Mennonite tradition:

> Since the sixteenth century, some Anabaptist groups have practiced foot washing in connection with the Lord's Supper. Typical of their general orientation away from the language of sacraments and rituals, they developed ethical interpretations of the action [but the emphasis shifted] . . . They ranged from the early role of establishing a strong sense of identity through an expression of cleansing, humility, discipleship, reconciliation, fellowship, and service. In our own time, the tendency among the Mennonite groups which practice foot washing is to emphasize reconciliation among themselves and active service to one another within the church.[8]

The hierarchical traditions continue, predominantly and ritually on Maundy Thursday. This is when the pope and some of his senior clerical associates wash the feet of several more in number of their junior clergy, in Rome: the superior serving his subordinates. This echoes elsewhere in the Roman Catholic Communion, as bishops ritually wash choirboys' feet in public acts of penitence and worship.

In Britain, some Anglican parishes and ecumenical gatherings annually acknowledge that *novum mandatum* as mutual foot washing occurs. In some places, this occurs as people gather before a Maundy Thursday Passover supper, sharing the bread and cup as Jesus would have done. Regrettably, in some British churches, foot washing on Maundy Thursday may be performed solemnly, but simply as a mime or dramatic rendering of John 13.

---

6. Dyck, ed., *Dirk Phillips*.

7. Krahn, *Dutch Anabaptism*.

8. Kreider, *Communion*, 286.

However, in Britain the most widely known rite of Maundy Thursday is the distribution, normally in a cathedral city, of Maundy money—a few precious metal coins—by the reigning monarch to a select number of well-deserving citizens. Both the value of the Maundy money and the number of people who receive it is exactly equivalent to the number of years for which that particular monarch has reigned. Again the *mandatum* is revealed in the service of a superior to their subordinates.

Because of a historic, cultural sacredness about feet—recall female foot binding—biblical foot washing has been lost to several oriental Christian movements. However, the contemporary Japanese Mennonite community practices an extensive, yet hardly ritualized form of hand washing between its members as an act of mutual service. Until Andrew personally experienced the induction practice of mutual hand washing as a hospice chaplain, this seemed hardly understandable as a sufficiently sacramental alternative to foot washing. This leaves us with a missional question: how far can the practice of foot washing be altered before it loses its John 13 new commandment imperative?

Reflecting Theologically

While the idea of a "superior ministering to their subordinates" in some form of ritual foot washing may be the predominantly known model of John 13's *novum mandatum*, it is biblically accurate as Jesus did not allow his disciples to wash his feet. Yet Jesus' example then does not feel as uncomfortable as much of contemporary practice does now, particularly when we recall Crossan's assessment of Jesus' movement as expressing a radical egalitarianism and an open commensality (see chapter 2).

It is the right of any, even every, inherited denomination, communion, or tradition to choose to do what they have already done. We believe that the *semper reformanda* (see Introduction) principle of our background means that we have seriously to cross-examine any Christian practice, to avoid that activity or ritual preserving us in an inexplicable aspic of "we have always done it this way."

We need to ask whether foot washing was just a practice of the Johannine Christian community.[9] The events of John 13 do not appear in the Synoptic Gospels. Arguments from silence are unhelpful. If we had only the Gospel accounts of the bread-and-cup moments of the Upper Room, we would be the poorer in our understanding but the Pauline Corinthian correspondence amplifies our thinking and spirituality. Graciously, in regard to foot washing,

9. Cullmann, *Johannine Circle*; Brown, *Community of the Beloved*.

we have the creative testimony of 1 Timothy 5:10, offering a clear list of the work of widows in a local Pauline Christian community.

While the ministry of foot washing by widows may have passed to the diaconate in the Western church, it became more ritualized, diluting its significance of both humility and mutuality, as a mark of Christian identity and community. Possibly inadvertently, this has led to a loss of understanding of its potentially sacramental intention by the watching church. Famously, Martin Luther, the magisterial Reformer, viewed foot washing as a ceremonial act—and for the majority of Reformed Church practice since, that view has remained.

The Anabaptist biblical scholar Lloyd Pieterson presented a creative academic paper to the UK's Easter 2018 Anabaptist Theology Forum, rethinking the theology of foot washing.[10] Pieterson offered us J. C. Thomas' insight: foot washing was a more widespread practice, and the Greek implies that the foot washing mentioned in 1 Timothy was a distinctly Christian act of humility, not just another aspect of household chores and hospitality, which is what the majority of commentators assume.[11]

In her *Communion Shapes Character*, Eleanor Kreider reflects upon her own Anabaptist-Mennonite foot-washing tradition:

> This will not be easy. In the footwashing rite, disciples take basins and towels and wash one another's feet, either in pairs or in sequence around a circle, each one washing the feet of the person next to them. After each washing, there is an embrace with a word of blessing. Such behavior is not a normal part of the life patterns of well-shod people in post-Christendom Europe and North America. For this reason, to some people the footwashing rite appears alien and unnatural; it is behavior that lacks ordinary analogues. To many, the footwashing rite elicits deep social discomfort; it seems an invasion of personal space, a "painfully intimate" encroachment upon another.[12]

Commenting upon this, Pieterson writes: "[The writers] go on to suggest that perhaps hand-washing should be substituted to mitigate the social unease but ask the question whether 'the sheer discomfort that many people feel at the thought of footwashing is a reason to take it seriously.'"[13] They conclude that a church practicing foot washing says four important things.

10. https://anabaptismtoday.co.uk/index.php/home/article/view/6/18.

11. Thomas, *Footwashing*, 135–36.

12. Kreider, *Communion*, 155–56.

13. Kreider and Kreider, *Worship and Mission*, 149.

- Jesus' words are authoritative for its life. A threefold exhortation is to be taken seriously no matter how uncomfortable it makes us.

- The rite is a gift with which we can play Jesus' story. As such it is socially subversive, turning the world upside down.

- The ritual is earthy and intimate. "Our feet are earthy, with their idiosyncratic calluses and odors. Our feet also are intimate—they are private, *our* business. But in the rite of footwashing, we vulnerably allow a fellow Christian to enter our space, our world of earth and intimacy."[14]

- The rite affects our life, transforming it to be one of reciprocity and service.

We share with Pieterson the observation that the mutuality of the footwashing experiences which the Kreiders describe in several books could be transformative for not just their own inherited denominational tradition. "The churches of post-Christendom, we believe, will rediscover foot-washing as a missional sacrament."[15]

Pieterson states, "It seems to me that footwashing has a claim to be regarded in a similar way to both baptism and Eucharist in the life of the church. The early Anabaptists seemed to think so too." We do not deny the validity of that claim but believe that Pieterson offers us far more in his exploration of foot washing as a "subversive ritual." For Pieterson, the mutuality of foot washing is mystagogical—the way Christian communities apprehend the rich patterns of God's Spirit in-breaking transformatively within worship, enabling participants to express this in ways akin to Christ's own practice.

The mutuality of foot washing challenges both the way of the world and those churches with hierarchies of clergy. It is subversive and transformative. Mutual and mystagogical foot washing has enriched the contemporary annual North American Mennonite-Catholic colloque, subverting its critics as it becomes an intentional practice in its participants' home congregations. "There is a mutuality of discipleship when all have to express their belonging to the church in the messy and awkward activity of footwashing!"[16] Such sacramental praxis is missional.

We should emphasize the important note struck by the Mennonite theologian-pastor John Rempel in his recent book about sacraments. There he offers a unified rite for combining foot washing with an *agape*, or "love-feast,"

14. Kreider and Kreider, *Worship and Mission*, 150–51.
15. Kreider and Kreider, *Worship and Mission*, 151.
16. O'Loughlin, *Washing Feet*, 144–46.

as part of a congregation's growth to the deeper fellowship and greater mutuality of service to one another.[17]

In Conclusion

During the first Christian millennium, foot washing was a rite often expressed privately, but in public worship it formed part of some unified rites of initiation. In the second millennium, it became far more associated with the rites of Maundy Thursday—and not always eucharistically. Only among the Radical Reformers did it gain acceptance as an ordinance, an activity which Christ commands of his followers. Such an act is sacramental at an *ex opera operato* level, meaning that the Holy Spirit works within the mutuality of the recipients to convey the grace of Christ. It is also an activity that emphasizes, through symbolic activity, the call of Christ to serve others within the messy reality of everyday life. Mutual foot washing is countercultural to a sanitized, individualistic Western lifestyle.

It is clear from this discussion that there are sacramental elements within the ritual act of foot washing. Within the context of worship, and using water as a signifier, it is an activity that acknowledges and marks both the covenantal relationship between God and those gathered, and their individual identities as members of their Christian community. While tradition dictates that this is not a "sacrament," there are without doubt those who would consider it a "moment of grace," through which a human-divine encounter takes place.

---

17. Rempel, *Recapturing*, Appendix 2.

11

Holy Places?

The way to Iona is arduous. In 597 CE, Columba and eleven monastic brothers were ejected from Ireland, drifting across the sea in open coracles until they arrived at the Scottish isle of Iona. There they founded the second major monastic settlement in Scotland; Ninian's *Candida Casa* at Whithorn, Galloway, was the first. Both were deemed "holy places," sending monks out on missionary journeys.

Around World War II, a charismatic Church of Scotland minister, George MacLeod, took unemployed Glasgow artisans and ordinands to pray and work together as they rebuilt the ruined Benedictine Iona Abbey and cloisters, while forging the nascent Iona Community. MacLeod described Iona as a "thin place, where earth and heaven collide."[1] For such a place to so facilitate sixth-century Irish monks, a later Benedictine foundation, and now a contemporary, globally known Christian community tells of recurring human-divine encounters in that special place. The American writer Daniel Taylor describes his wonder in exploring Iona and other such ancient sacredly Christian Irish and British sites;[2] and it is also true that those visiting Iona today regularly share that same sense of the island being a "thin place."[3]

There is something innately human about the search for, and establishment of, sacred places, both within the natural and constructed world. The campaign by Aboriginal Australians to keep people from climbing the sacred rock Uluru (renamed Ayres Rock by European interlopers), and the battle to

1. Ferguson, *George MacLeod*.

2. Taylor, *Sacred Places*.

3. Andrew has visited or stayed on Iona more than twenty times and can affirm that the shared "thin place" experience of life there for many often elicits the description as sacramental.

preserve the natural heritage of Native American reserves, combine with ar-cheological evidence to demonstrate that the relatedness between particular places and sacred experience dates back millennia.

It is impossible for contemporary spiritual searchers to know the pur-pose for constructing huge statues on Easter Island in the mid-Pacific, or the raison d'être for the stone circles and long barrows near Concarneau, Brittany (France), at Avebury and Stonehenge in southern England, and at Macchu Pichu in Peru.[4] Yet there is no doubt that those who built them experienced them as places where heaven and earth met, just as those who gather to wor-ship in buildings like the Sagrada Familia in Barcelona or at St Paul's Basilica at the Vatican, do today.

Bishop John Inge has asked how places can be sacramental, but does not advocate "place as sacrament."[5] Inge and Taylor join many other writers of the past generation connecting spirituality, sacredness, and place. We as writers continue to wonder whether place can be a sacrament. If it can, is that limited only to geographic locations, or can it include humanity's religious structures, too?

Rethinking Holy Places

In his book *God and the Enchantment of Place*, David Brown argues that, throughout the history of the church, "the sacramental" has been too narrowly defined.[6] If God is at work everywhere, he argues, why shouldn't human-divine encounter take place in contexts beyond the church?[7] Brown's detailed and sometimes overcomplicated examination of the case for "re-enchantment" draws mainly on the work of the sociologist Max Weber, and philosophers Plato, Plotinus, and Martin Heidegger. He argues that the Enlightenment and consequential advance of rationality have caused the loss of "medieval un-derstandings of sacrament [that] were intimately intwined with magic, [and] from which the Reformation in both its major forms successfully extricated itself." The result, he argues, has been "the disenchantment of the world," a phrase first used by the German philosopher, Friedrich Schiller.[8]

Re-enchantment is only possible, argues Brown, if the church's un-derstanding of human-divine encounter extends beyond current narrow

---

4. Francis, *Spirituality and the Land*.

5. Inge, *Christian Theology of Place*.

6. Brown, *God and the Enchantment of Place*.

7. Brown, *God and the Enchantment of Place*, 6–8.

8. Brown, *God and the Enchantment of Place*, 17.

definitions, "acknowledging the fact that God might speak not only through biblical revelation but also through implicit promises given in the way the world has been made."[9] Brown suggests that: "Sport, drama, humour, dance, architecture, place and home, the natural world are all part of a long list of activities and forms of experience that have been relegated to the periphery of religious reflection, but which once made invaluable contributions to a human perception that this world is where God can be encountered, and encountered often."[10]

Using various forms of art, including iconography, Brown illustrates the different ways God can be seen at work in the world, visually and experientially as well as through symbols and words. With regard to place specifically, he cities Heidegger, for whom "dwelling" and "being" are intimately connected.

Reflecting on the Biblical Peoples

As we have shown in previous chapters, there is biblical precedent for almost all activities which might be considered sacramental. The subject of "place" is no different. In the Hebrew Scriptures:

- The first relational encounter between God and humans is set in the garden of Eden, and it is Adam and Eve's exile from that garden which marks the beginning of humanity's fallen existence.

- When God reconciles with the people by rescinding the flood, the location of the ark is given as on Mount Ararat.

- It is at Bethel that Abram first builds an altar and communes with God, Jacob wrestles with the angel, and from where the judges deliver their judgments.

- Mount Sinai is the place where Moses receives the Ten Commandments.

- It is from Mount Carmel that Elijah begins to facilitate the return of the people of God from the worship of Baal.

Without exception all of these places are considered holy, places where an altar is constructed and incense burned, so that the division between heaven and earth thins, and God becomes present in the midst of the people.

This is even more marked in the witness to the incarnation of Jesus that is the divine embodiment in the world, as revealed in the apostolic writings. The Gospels mark a fundamental change in the way place is utilized. Mountains

9. Brown, *God and the Enchantment of Place*, 21.

10. Brown, *God and the Enchantment of Place*, 9.

are still important—but now they become the locations for Jesus' central teaching and miracles, particularly the Sermon on the Mount and consequent feeding miracle. The two paramount experiences are the transfiguration and ascension. In the first the disciples unwittingly attempt to build a tabernacle, and are warned by Jesus that it is not necessary—for God is already present among them. Similarly during the ascension Jesus teaches, then leaves the disciples, commissioning them—not to remain in that holy place, but to leave the mountainside to go and await the coming of the Holy Spirit.

Pentecost marks, once and for all, the end of the need for the building of altars and the burning of incense—for Jesus will himself be present with each one of them (and us): "until the end of the age."

Christian Sacralization and Place

During the Christendom period, Christians had a tendency to sacralize a place of previous religious or pagan significance. One such is the ancient Irish hill of Tara, with its Neolithic passages and ruins, where the high king of Ireland presided over the rulers of Ireland's four provinces. For nearly 900 years, there has been a church dedicated to St. Patrick on that hillside; legend tells that this was so God could personally bless the high king. Even Iona's now-ruined Augustinian nunnery has the pagan *sheela na gig* motif carved into its wall, indicating previous belief patterns. Many English churchyards and monastic houses were deliberately enclosed, or were built upon former pagan "holy places" in order to sacralize the land in the name of the Christian God.[11]

However, "sacralizing the land" does not result in the land, or any place, becoming a "sacrament." Such things have been said about Northern Ireland's Corrymeela Community (Gael.: hill of harmony), which became a reconciling seedbed and force for peace for both Protestants and Catholics during "the troubles."[12] The numerous testimonies of healing and transformative prayer at *Ffald-y-Brenin* (Welsh: Sheepfold of the King) in southwest Wales often assign a sacramental witness. But none of these makes "place" a sacrament. Our point here is to demonstrate the ubiquity of such sacramental experience as described to us by others in contemporary generations.

All these experiences are very different and the way in which one calibrates those experiences are not the same—and certainly not our criteria. Andrew found great spiritual if not sacramental succor throughout a turbulent

11. Two other extant famous examples are the Catholic church on top of the Neolithic burial mound in Carnac, Brittany, or the planting of a dissenters' chapel almost at the heart of the Mesolithic Avebury stone circle in the 1660s.

12. McCreary, *In War and Peace*.

period of ministry from almost daily attendance at evensong in a quiet, darkened parish church; but this was an individual experience. No doubt there are many across Britain and the world who have had unique and special sacramental moments in cathedrals, back-street chapels, and declared retreat houses, as we have too. But this does not make them "sacraments."

The "After Christendom" Challenge

With the decline of Christianity as a practiced religion over the past fifty years or so, the concept of places as holy and buildings as sacred has changed, certainly within the English context. We have followed tourists around historic English cathedrals, who demonstrate little knowledge of the sacred understandings these spaces invoke for worshipers over many centuries. In England it is more likely that a committed soccer fan will venerate their team's stadium than any nearby church building. Yet, while church attendance continues to diminish, the greatest rise in numbers at public worship in the past fifteen years is in cathedrals and, while the general downward trend continues, numbers attending cathedrals, particularly for festival services, are holding their own.[13]

Majestic, ancient, holy buildings still hold magnetic pull, both for Christians and non-Christians. However, churches with a greater mission focus logically attract more newcomers, adherents, and ultimately believers. The experience of the UK's New Church movement in the final quarter of the twentieth century demonstrates that, as they were planted from homes into schools, community halls, and even industrial premises, vibrant Christianity was no longer always associated with historic or sacred spaces. Experience, and not place, was becoming more important.[14]

From the 1990s on, the "emerging church" movement,[15] and accompanying Fresh Expressions initiative, have resulted in churches being planted even more creatively. Locations have included limiting themselves to people's own homes,[16] and meeting in everything from commercial kitchens[17] to pubs, with huge fluidity in what traditionalists might call "liturgy" and worship. Sacraments do not always feature high on their agenda, and when they do the issue of who will preside at them often causes tension. It is the gathering of

---

13. Church of England, *Cathedral Statistics 2018*.

14. Walker, *Restoring the Kingdom*.

15. E.g., Gibbs and Bolger, *Emerging Churches*.

16. Banks and Banks, *Church Comes Home*; Francis, *Eat, Pray, Tell*.

17. Glasson, *Mixed-up Blessing*.

people and what they experience together, rather than the place where they meet, that is important.

One surprising response to the COVID-19 pandemic has been the vitriolic debate in social media—now public too—about places as sacred spaces. In rural southwest France (where Andrew ran a retreat house) and southern Ireland, there have been howls of protest that church buildings have been locked down so that, even without any public liturgy, those spaces cannot be used for personal silent prayer during Holy Week. In the Netherlands, Germany, and Britain "online services" offered by solo church leaders have provoked much news media comment about the lack of access to "much loved" places of worship for others. In the UK, one newspaper misreported a disagreement between Bishop Sarah Mullally of London and Archbishop Justin Welby about which congregational leaders could stream worship from their consecrated buildings, whether with or without congregants.[18] If these criticisms were all from frequently attending activist Christians, one might understand the protests, but how much damage has such a lockdown done to those critical yet spiritual seekers for whom "place" might be a necessary stepping stone into faith?

This brief summary of the relationship between people and their buildings does demonstrate that, while there is a role for place to play in creating a context where sacramental experiences or activities might take place, it is far from clear that the places are in themselves sacramental, and certainly they should not be described as "sacraments."

Pilgrims and Places

Since biblical days, people have been journeying to God's special place; what was the promised land to the Hebrew people if not God's special place? As a boy, Jesus was left behind in Jerusalem, having been taken there by his earthly parents. Was not this a pilgrimage to the holy city of the Jews? Was Jesus' final journey to "celebrate the Passover in Jerusalem" just a piece of divine stage management in the salvation narrative? The *Kumbh Mela*[19] in India or the Islamic necessity of *haj*—pilgrimage to Mecca—tell us that, across faiths, people become pilgrims to journey to places of human-divine encounter.

Between us, we have led youth pilgrimages to Taizé and Iona, as well as ecumenical groups to Israel, Lindisfarne, Lourdes, and Rome. We have

18. "Bishops disagree over online worship," *Daily Telegraph*, April 7 2020.

19. Regarded by UNESCO as "the largest religious gathering of people," this twelve-yearly Hindu pilgrimage to four riverside sites involves literally millions ritually bathing at the same time in preparation for prayers.

accompanied others along the English Pilgrims Way (from Winchester to Canterbury) and walked much of the 500-mile Camino de Santiago trail. In the last generation, numbers attempting that Santiago pilgrimage have grown tenfold.

No longer is pilgrimage locked in medieval Chaucer or undertaken as a Catholic penance. As pilgrimage is embraced afresh, it is not just the destination but the journey's route which becomes symbolic of the human-divine encounter for many participants. While the journey may be corporate, the human-divine encounters tend to be so individualistic that they can hardly satisfy anyone's formal understanding of them as a sacrament.

While individual expectations, realizations, and experience of pilgrimage are such that some may claim the journey has been "sacramental," pilgrimage is not a "sacrament." However, we do have to recognize that pilgrimage through God's creation to a holy site is part of an emerging new spirituality for both Christian believers and seekers, during which the human-divine encounter is often apparent.

In Conclusion

David Brown's *Enchantment* premise is that it is by interpreting sacramentality through place that God's immanence and transcendence are most fully revealed. In any examination of the human-divine encounter this theology is helpful, as it enables us *all* individually to examine the nature of the God we encounter.

This thinking is further helped by the series of essays, *Sacred Place*, edited by Holm and Bowker, which outlines the views of different faiths about holiness and the importance of certain places. In our conversations during the writing of this book, several people referred to the sacraments as their "pillars of faith." Only Islam includes the *haj* or sacred pilgrimage as one of its five essential pillars of faith. While historically there has been a connection made between the act of pilgrimage and penance, it has never been deemed a sacrament throughout the history of Christian belief; and with this we concur.

Each of us (as writers) has associations with particular sacred buildings, which have enabled us individually to have recurring human-divine encounters—but this has not been true for everyone who visits those buildings. There is an importance of place when interpreting the validity of (our) "context" criteria.

Davies, who wrote the "Christianity" chapter of Holm and Bowker's volume, explicitly notes: "One key to understanding the difference between Christians happy to have sacred places and those unhappy with the idea lies in the sacraments and the emphasis placed upon the sacraments and upon an authorised priesthood trained to administer them."[20]

In other words, the more sacramental in tradition a particular community of faith, and the greater the emphasis on an ordained priesthood, the more likely they are to acknowledge, identify, and revere sacred or holy places. Davies's assumption seems to be that if people already venerate transformative human-divine encounters, they will also be more accepting of "sacred spaces." Yet the Roman Catholic Church never declared that particular holy spaces should be sacraments.

The two previous chapters have highlighted the importance of context in providing a setting for human-divine encounters, in terms of both physical setting and community focus. However, this does not make either of them "sacraments." It is not solely the setting in which an activity takes place which makes it a sacrament, or even sacramental, although the setting clearly has a role to play in creating the right context for that activity.

20. Davies, "Christianity," 52.

Part Three

Encountering God after Christendom

12

Encountering God: Discipleship and Spirituality

For some Christians, the term *spirituality* is a source of consternation. Understood and practiced in many different ways, it deals with matters of the heart and soul, reaching into the deepest fathoms of self-identity. For some it remains deeply personal, or even avoided as a topic; for others life is not complete unless they are regularly seeing a spiritual director.

Discipleship as a term, while less contentious, is also understood and out-worked in different ways, being as it is the practical consequence of a person's spirituality. Some might describe discipleship as an activity, a way of expressing a deep faith through community service or campaigning for social justice, for example. For others it is more of an attitude, a way of seeing the world. Still others see the life of discipleship as orthopraxy: it cannot be compartmentalized into activities and attitudes. Everything they believe, think, say, and do is understood to be a consequence of their faith in and relationship with Christ.

Therefore while spirituality and discipleship are intimately connected, they are not the same thing. They are, however, shaped within the life of the individual according to a number of factors, not least of which is the way in which they encounter God.

The Human-Divine Encounter

We have already seen that, since biblical times, believers have participated in both individual and corporate activities which enable them to enter into human-divine encounter. Whether it be through the building of a shrine and burning incense, making sacrifices, ritual bathing or, more latterly, sharing bread and wine around a table, it is clear that all these corporate activities have one common feature: they are participated in by individuals who iden-tify with them in a particular way. How these "particular ways" are practiced and understood are contingent on the context, tradition, and the covenantal understanding within which they are set, and it is through these activities in turn that individual and corporate identity emerges.

It is through a human-divine encounter that God gives Moses the Ten Commandments and the other laws which enable the Hebrews to form a structured community with a defined set of beliefs. It is through the provi-sion and sharing of food that Jesus demonstrates his authority, divinity, and identity, providing the disciples with the stimulus to form the earliest Chris-tian communities. Much later, during the Reformation, in challenging the understanding of what was acceptable sacramental practice, the Anabaptists demonstrated their beliefs, forming the mutually supportive fellowships that enabled them to stand firm in the face of persecution.

Spirituality, discipleship, and sacramentality are therefore inextricably linked. Furthermore the nature of the relationship between individual partici-pants and corporate identity, expressed through sacramental practice, is both reflexive and strongly contingent.

The sacramental theologian Louis Marie Chauvet suggests that the de-velopment of the Christian life is achieved within the context of the church through three interrelated activities: *kerygma* (God's revelation mediated through Scripture), *leiturgia* (the set forms of words and associated activities used in worship, e.g., sacraments), and *diakonia* (Christian service, the root of the term *deacon,* whose role it is to serve the community on behalf of the church). For Chauvet the consequence of these three activities is itself three-fold: knowledge, gratitude, and action. While Chauvet clearly writes from a particular perspective—one can almost sense the Roman Catholic practice of touching the head, heart, and lips in response to the declaration of Christ's love—there is strong merit in his suggestion that what takes place within the context of worship and the activities that follow it are intimately related.

Take the celebration of Holy Communion as an example. Through the eucharistic act participants are drawn into the experience of becoming part of the body of Christ, are fed by the "body of Christ," and are challenged to *be* "the body of Christ" in and for the world. This anamnetic activity, cele-brated within church tradition and embodying the covenant understanding of human-divine encounter, empowers and enables individuals to live out their life of discipleship, confirmed in their identity as people of Christ.[1]

Holy Communion is, however, just one example of the *leiturgia* used in worship. A liturgy—whether it be set or extemporized, and experienced

---

1. Chauvet, *Sacraments*; Chauvet, *Symbol and Sacrament.*

through words, music, or symbolic actions—has a number of forms. What the activity consists of is perhaps less relevant than its purpose and expected outcome. The singing of charismatic worship songs is, for some, as spiritual and revelatory an experience as sharing bread and wine. Those nurtured within the context of Book of Common Prayer worship find a freedom in the set words through which Christ becomes present for them by the power of the Holy Spirit. The practice of foot washing, usually included in the Maundy service the day before Good Friday, demonstrates both the servanthood of Jesus and his call to Christians themselves to be servants in the world. All of these corporate activities serve the purpose of forging among participants a sense of common identity, as well as nourishing them spiritually and equipping them emotionally to go into the world as Jesus' disciples.

Understanding Spiritual Development

As we have already seen, the ways in which Christian spirituality is defined and developed are as varied as the numbers of "church communions" around the world throughout history. It is therefore impossible to conclude that any one pattern of sacramental practice, or even the need for "sacraments" themselves, is necessary for spiritual development and the consequential call to discipleship. A more useful approach might be to understand the process by which spiritual development takes place, then assess the role of sacramental practice in it.

Modeling spiritual development within a Christian faith context was first attempted by an American professor of marketing, James Engel, together with his colleague, Wil Norton, and published in their 1975 book, *What's Gone Wrong with the Harvest?*[2] The "Engel Scale" describes how individuals come to faith in eight stages. In 1976 the United Church of Christ-turned-Episcopal pastor and theologian, John H. Westerhoff, in *Will Our Children Have Faith?*[3] proposed just four stages of faith which loosely correlate with the principles of developmental psychology. A number of different models followed, the most notable being James Fowler's *Stages of Faith*,[4] and psychiatrist M. Scott Peck's "Stages of Spiritual Development" as described in *The Different Drum: Community-making and Peace.*[5] While each has its own particularities, the different models have a level of commonality:

2. Engel and Norton, *What's Gone Wrong.*
3. Westerhoff, *Will Our Children.*
4. Fowler, *Stages of Faith.*
5. Peck, *Different Drum.*

- They all assume that people are born with an implicit awareness of a "supreme being" but no framework within which to set it (Engel and Norton). Peck describes this period as "chaotic, disordered and reckless," while Fowler says it is "primal or undifferentiated."

- During their childhood years those brought up as Christians attain a basic understanding of the faith and adopt a collection of associated understandings and behaviors, termed by Peck as "Blind Faith." This is where, for some, faith development stalls or stops altogether (Fowler).

- By late adolescence most people will begin to develop an "individuative-reflective" approach (Fowler) or "skepticism" (Peck), causing them to enter a "searching faith" period (Westerhoff).

- Throughout adulthood, a gradual process of development takes place, with the majority practicing a "conjunctive" faith (Fowler), incorporation into the faith (Engel and Norton), or an "owned faith" (Westerhoff). This is characterized by reaching beyond knowledge to an experiential, more spiritually focused faith.

- A minority will pursue a deeper spirituality, described by Peck as "mystical," by Engel and Norton as "Communion with God," and by Fowler as "universalizing."

First, these writers assume that the starting point is an "awareness of a supreme being"; second, that spiritual development is a linear, chronological process correlating with physical age; and third, that faith development comes to a point where it moves beyond knowledge to experience, rendering participants open to traditions beyond their own. Only one of the volumes under survey uses phraseology that might refer to sacramental practice. Engel and Norton's "repentance and faith" stage followed by "new birth" could equate with the point at which believers' baptism or confirmation/chrism are celebrated. Their final stage, "communion with God," has eucharistic implications. Interestingly these two stages are the most striking and experiential steps, requiring a change of heart rather than just a gradual logical response to the gathering of knowledge.

It is notable that all of the modelers are white, Protestant, well-educated men, writing from within a North American "Christendom" context. It is understandable, therefore, that their observations will be in line with this experience, as well as the experience of the white, well-educated, British authors of this book! A notable absence in the modelers' writing is any reference to the activity of the Holy Spirit. In addition any reference they make to sacramental behavior, albeit implied, focuses on the two sacraments of baptism and Holy Communion. However, this discussion concerns not what constitutes a "sacrament," but the role the sacramental might play in the development of individual spirituality. The models provide a helpful framework, despite their limitations.

We have already noted, through the work of Chauvet, that the Christian life is achieved through revelation, experience, and activity, embodied in three interrelated activities, *kerygma*, *leiturgia*, and *diakonia*. By setting the characteristics associated with the different stages of faith alongside these ecclesial activities, it is possible to see how sacramentality might best be expressed differently at different stages, and the extent to which that sacramental practice influences spiritual development and/or discipleship. As the models have so much in common, it seems pertinent to choose one framework on which to focus.

A New Way of Calibrating?

A strength of Fowler's modeling is that it takes seriously the changes in the way people view the world and learn according to their age. This makes it very practical. Faith—which Fowler contrasts with belief—is integral to every area of life, and the way in which it is applied is an important aspect of both spirituality and discipleship. The framework gives parameters against which it is possible to explore how *kerygma*, *diakonia*, and, particularly for the purposes of this study, *leiturgia* are used within current church practice.

Fowler suggests that spiritual development has seven stages. During the first, "undifferentiated" stage, an infant can do little more than experience comfort or discomfort. It is not until the ability to comprehend language begins that he or she progresses to the "intuitive-projective" stage, "an imitative phase in which the child can be powerfully and permanently influenced by examples, moods, actions and stories of the visible faith of primally related adults."[6] From the age of about seven years, the child enters a "mythical-literal" phase, during which they begin to develop a belief framework. At this point the concept of God is generally anthropomorphic, and metaphors and symbols are taken literally. Adolescence usually correlates with the "synthetic-conventional" stage, characterized by a desire to conform to authority and

---

6. http://www.theinterfaithobserver.org/journal-articles/2017/1/2/stuck-on -the-spiritual-spectrum.

to belong. In early adulthood an individual reaches Stage 4—the "individua-tive-reflective" stage—during which he or she takes responsibility for beliefs and feelings, and becomes open to understanding complexity and conflict. Stage 5, generally reached from the mid-thirties, results in an openness to paradox, transcendence, compassion, and "the acceptance of unexplainable multidimensional truths." For many this is the final stage, with only a minority reaching Stage 6, the period of enlightenment, during which the individual concerned enters an awareness of universalism and focus on the principles of love and justice.

Having identified these stages as the parameters against which to measure the efficacy of *kerygma* (how revelation is mediated), *leiturgia* (the language, means or activity used), and *diakonia* (the resultant sense of call to service), it is now necessary to create descriptors for each stage. These descriptors can then be used to assess whether current sacramental understandings reflect, or counter, spiritual development, both individually and corporately, among people in churches. Suggestions can also be made about how the revelation of God's word is best mediated, the activities which best enable the presence of Christ to be experienced, and the sort of discipleship that might then be encouraged.

Table 12.1 demonstrates how, at each stage of faith, particular activities or means of mediation might appropriately be adopted in order to facilitate spiritual development. Against each of Fowler's stages is a summary of the characteristics associated with that particular level of faith development, and accompanying suggestions of the sorts of activities which might be ap-propriate for an individual of that age and accompanying stage of faith. We have taken the liberty of categorizing these activities under the headings of *kerygma*, *leiturgia*, and *diakonia* according to which of the parameters the activity best fits.

TABLE 12.1. ACTIVITIES WHICH MIGHT BE USED TO FACILITATE
SPIRITUAL DEVELOPMENT IN ACCORDANCE WITH FOWLER'S
"STAGES OF FAITH" MODEL

Stage	Age	Name	Characteristics	*Kerygma*	*Leiturgia*	*Diakonia*
0	0–2	Undifferentiated	Consistent nurture vs negative experience = trust, sense of safety	Comfort	Touch	Nurture
1	3–7	Intuitive-Projective	Exposure to unconscious, fluidity of thought patterns	Play	Stories play	Contact with people
2	7–12	Mythical-Literal	Strong belief in justice/reciprocity of universe, deities anthropomorphic; metaphors/symbols taken literally	Stories, discussion	Images things	Desire for justice
3	12+?	Synthetic-Conventional	Conformity to authority and religions, development of personal identity. Conflicts ignored (can't handle inconsistency)	Learning via age-appropriate media	Introduction of formal liturgies/practices	Activities to make a practical difference
4	21+?	Individuative-Reflective	Taking responsibility for beliefs/feelings and reflecting on them; openness to new complexities, but also awareness of conflict in beliefs	Learning via age appropriate media	Continuity of formal liturgy/practices but with exploration	Local service or campaign for justice
5	35+?	Conjunctive	Acknowledge paradox and transcendence; resolve conflicts; acceptance of unexplainable multidimensional truths	Spiritual exploration	Experiential/meaningful sacramental activity	Practical and symbolic discipleship
6	45+?	Universalizing	Enlightenment, characterized by: compassion; community; people—as from a universal community—should be treated with universal principles of love and justice	Deepening spiritual exploration	Encounter with Christ through sacramental activity	Practical and symbolic discipleship

For example, Table 12.1 suggests that, for a five-year-old at the first stage of faith development (intuitive-projective) the best means of mediation are through play, the telling of stories, and human contact. Experience will tell any parent that to expect a five-year-old to sit quietly, listen to a sermon, and take away from it a fuller understanding of God's word is entirely unreasonable. Nor will a five-year-old have the capacity to take in the meaning of a eucharistic prayer or understand the meaning and purpose of an ordination service.

However, this does not mean that all "sacramental" activities are beyond that five-year-old's reach. Those who invite children to participate in the sharing of Holy Communion will be able to relate instances where the eyes of a child, receiving a piece of bread during the Eucharist, glow with joy as they experience being one of the "chosen," a true member of the body of Christ. In addition their desire to go then and share that experience with others is perfectly natural.

One thing Fowler's "stages of faith framework" fails to engage with is the importance of experiential learning for children growing up after Christendom. Indeed it is a fundamental weakness of the model for, in the early to mid-twenty-first century, children learn by absorption through experience, not by rote. A simple example of this is early stage mathematics. English five-year-olds learn math using number blocks. By moving them round, building towers of different heights, and by separating them out, the children learn to add, subtract, multiply, and divide. When necessary they use fingers. It would be unusual these days to see a child using a linear method.

The activities we have listed in Table 12.1 are those we would consider appropriate "after Christendom." Where Fowler might have expected *kerygma* at Stages 3 and 4 to involve hearing sermons and engaging in traditional Bible study, our list suggests instead that it will involve "learning via age-appropriate media." While this might seem somewhat non-prescriptive, we felt it necessary to give a definition which enables the incorporation of a variety of communication media: from Zoom online gatherings to YouTube videos, as well as the traditional spoken and written word.

A further point to note from Table 12.1 is how the activities in the *diakonia* column flow from the *leiturgia* column. Mediation through touch in the "undifferentiated" stage is followed by discipleship through contact with others in proceeding years. The use of "images and things" liturgically or sacramentally for a seven-to-twelve-year-old leads to discipleship of a practical nature in the following years. While it might be stretching the point to say that it is a logical conclusion, the typology suggests that sacramental or liturgical practice might have an impact on the later call to discipleship.

There is a logic to anointing an infant, for through the medium of touch the child experiences the warmth and safety that accompanies the activity. There is merit in exploring with men and women in their early twenties how they wish to celebrate the sacraments to make them a more meaningful encounter with Christ within their own context, tradition, and covenantal understanding. The point here is not to try to work out a definitive list of which activities should be described as "sacraments," and where they fit within the "stage of faith" model. It is instead to understand how best to practice those which, according to the context, tradition, covenantal understanding, and identities of those participating, best represent or signify the mediated love of Christ in-breaking into the ordinary in extraordinary ways.

There are two important caveats to using Fowler's framework as a tool. The first is a logical consequence of how the stages are described by Fowler himself. Each stage is given both a name and an approximate age at which it will be reached. It is clear that the "+?" he includes means that there is some movement in when or whether these developments take place.

This means two things: first, the categories are a movable feast. Not only do people reach different stages at different times in their lives, but also there will be some for whom the stages just do not correlate with their experience. This makes analysis more complicated than it might first seem. It is not enough to say, "Someone who is thirty-five will be at a conjunctive stage both in faith and emotional/psychological development, and will therefore relate to experiential sacramental activity." Each person has their own identity and set of criteria for how they practice their faith (or not), and their own preferences as to how they wish to celebrate the sacraments.

The second caveat, already rehearsed to a certain extent, is the "Christendom" factor. Activities and traditions which, until the turn of the last century, had been adequate to nurture and challenge believers in their faith, are now no longer working. This is why the spiritual development frameworks were included in books with titles such as *Will Our Children Have Faith?*, *What's Gone Wrong with the Harvest?*, and *The Different Drum*. Since these books were written it is not only the children of church members who have chosen not to engage with the Christian faith; it is their grandchildren too. It is estimated that, in the UK, we are in the third generation of people who have no church background, who do not exist under the "sacred canopy" of Christian narrative and all the assumptions that go with it.[7] Is it even reasonable, then, to use a table based on an outdated framework to suggest a new way of thinking about the sacraments? Only the reader can answer that!

While it is by no means appropriate to suggest that this exercise solves the age-old conflict over the who, what, when, where, and how of sacramental theology and practice, it can assist theologians and practitioners in thinking through the nature of their sacramental practice. It is no longer good enough

7. Berger, *Sacred Canopy.*

simply to say, "This is what we do, this is what it means, and this is when you qualify."

Spirituality, Discipleship, and the Holy Spirit

As already mentioned, perhaps the greatest flaw in Fowler's model—and this chapter—it might be argued, is that there is virtually no mention of the activity of the Holy Spirit! As already stated, the modeling of the stages of faith as described above is set within a Protestant context where the activity of the Holy Spirit is understood to have been assumed into the structures and authority of the church. This leaves little room for radical conversion and any form of spiritual fervor. Fowler's stages of faith assume that one has to get to Stage 6 before one has the possibility of entering an "enlightenment" period, with its focus on the principles of love and justice. The term *Enlightenment* itself is one often used synonymously with early modernity. It is not so much a radical conversion that Fowler expects here; more a gradual awakening or gentle switching on of a lightbulb.

For those whose conversion has been a charismatic, life-changing experience, Fowler's model simply does not work. Nor would it be relevant to those whose experience in a Pentecostal or charismatic culture, similar to Fowler's "enlightenment" stage, occurs early on in their Christian journey. Consider, for example, the experience of John Newton, the slave trader who wrote the hymn "Amazing Grace." He was a declared Christian; yet he condoned, perpetuated, and even encouraged the trading of people as commodities. His was a radical moment of conversion, during a storm when he thought he would die. One could describe that conversion experience, one that deconstructed his worldview and remade it in a new likeness, as a moment of "enlightenment." His new reality wasn't just a case of focusing on the principles of love and justice: it was to go out and transform that which he had previously actively perpetuated. From that human-divine encounter, the call to discipleship which flowed can be described as nothing less than miraculous.

Newton's experience was not "sacramental" in terms of church practice. But it was a human-divine encounter, a "moment of grace," which changed him forever. As Christians we should never be surprised when the Holy Spirit sweeps in, just as she did on the day of Pentecost, changing hearts and transforming minds. No model in the world can legislate for that—nor should it. And in a time when a church culture that facilitates sound catechetical structures is less and less effective, perhaps we will need to rely more and more on the Holy Spirit to provide transformative "moments of grace." Such a need opens wide again the discussion concerning how sacraments and sacramental acts are defined. For the Holy Spirit cannot be contained, nor her efficacy doubted. This brings us back to the question we posed at the beginning of the book: how might sacramental theology and practice best be shaped for the future?

13

Sacraments after Christendom?

We have already seen that, despite their usefulness, the "stages of faith" models are in some ways fit only for yesterday. Are they still relevant for a generation in which far fewer people committedly attend church? We have explored at length sacramental praxis as it is seen through our eyes and those of others, and have introduced models that we believe might assist other Christians in doing the same. In this penultimate chapter we wish to delve a bit deeper into what we mean by the term "after Christendom" and how it applies to sacramental theology and practice.

What Kind of "After Christendom"?

So far, we have spoken of "after" or "post-" Christendom as a uniform entity; clearly it is not. We have been writing predominantly about Latin Christendom. Crudely, this was the Latin-speaking church in its northward expansion from the Levant and the Mediterranean, over many centuries, and its Western European successors. In its later colonializing turn, this covers the English-speaking territory of Australia, Ireland, and North America as well as the UK.

The political theologian John Heathershaw, a UK professor of international relations, suggests that "Christendom," rather than being a factual reality, is the consequence of an "imagining"—a particular way of seeing the world.[1] Of course there are as many ways of seeing the world as there are people on the planet, and for the majority of the people on this planet "Christendom," as we understand it in the English-speaking West, is an "imagining" that makes very little sense at all. Having said that, the world as *we* authors

1. Heathershaw, *Security after Christendom*, chapters 1–4.

"imagine" it has, until recently, very much been a Christendom one; and it is from this perspective that we write. Heathershaw helpfully identifies three different forms of Christendom:

- "Centered Christendom": Historically, Latin Christendom is a strong example of this, in which church and state integrally collaborate in both their support for one another and the suppression, even violent, of any dissent or alternative belief. We can identify this in the twelfth-century Crusades or the sixteenth-century Reformation. This creates trade and geopolitical isolation.

- "Decentered Christendom": This could describe the Western democracies of Latin Christendom since World War II. It is typified by widespread toleration, increasing religious plurality, and statutory relaxation of previous Christian norms (e.g., marriage and divorce). The church has decreasing power to restrain the state's agenda and acceptance/appeasement of other faith or secular agendas becomes common.

- "Recentered Christendom": Such as those in both secularized France and post-Communist Russia in which the State is supreme, accepting conditional support from Christians and other faiths. By actively accepting interfaith dialogues, individual faith is subsumed by the secular agenda and the crossing of ideological boundaries to create trade links or geopolitical advantage.[2]

Each has its particularities, but essentially they describe the ways the church and state relate to each other.

These "imagined" forms of Christendom are by no means static: indeed, "imagined Christendom" could be used as a fourth category to describe individual nations at times of ideological transition and political upheaval. During such times, a strong church can engage in the power vacuum to influence future social, political, and creative development. Despite some flaws, Greece with its Orthodox Church in the years following the 1974 ending of the military junta, when Andrew traveled extensively there annually, offers an example.

We would argue that the United Kingdom is in a period of "imagining"; indeed it can be argued that each of the countries that make up the UK is going through its own "imagining" process. It is currently unclear whether England is in a period of "recentered Christendom," or whether the church now has so little influence that it cannot even entertain a civic or public role in the future, and thus cannot claim to exist within a form of "Christendom" at all.

---

2. Heathershaw, *Security after Christendom*, chapters 1–4.

Whichever is the case, for the purposes of our discussion, this categorization of different forms of Christendom is relevant for two reasons; first, a reader in most English-speaking locations can identify the shifts within their own nation of religious attitudes and the church's role in the state. Second, during a period when society is transitioning from one form of Christendom to another (or indeed into post-Christendom), a more fluid response to newcomers exploring the Christian faith is needed.

Developing Sacramental Understanding During a Period of "Imagining"

Having defined what we mean by the term *after Christendom*, we now turn to exploring how our current "imagining" might apply to sacramental theology and practice. To do this we will be using our previously identified typology (symbol, covenant, tradition, identity, and context), using a worked example from a description of sacramental theology presented by the well-known British Anglican priest and commentator, Angela Tilby.[3]

The description appears in an article published during the COVID-19 pandemic in April 2020. Tilby discusses whether it is appropriate to celebrate the Eucharist as part of an online gathering during a time of lockdown. She sums up her sacramental theology clearly and concisely using only a few hundred words.

She starts by quoting the Bishop of Western Louisiana, who had written to his diocese stating that consecrating bread and/or wine "virtually" (meaning digitally, over the internet) "exceeds the recognized bounds set by our rubrics and inscribed in our (Episcopal) theology of the Eucharist." Tilby agrees with him. For her it is appropriate to celebrate the Eucharist only when a Christian community is physically together and, should such an act be conducted with an online gathering, "the bread is not truly broken because it was never truly united." She suggests that Christians "honour the Eucharist best not by insisting that it is our right to consume, but by honouring the space that separates us."

What is so interesting about this article, for the purposes of this discussion, are the numerous assumptions behind what Tilby (and indeed the Bishop of Western Louisiana whom she quotes) writes.

First, it is assumed that one person has the authority, under Christ, to dictate how and when the sacraments can be celebrated. Second, Tilby

---

3. https://www.churchtimes.co.uk/articles/2020/24-april/comment/columnists/angela-tilby-virtual-bread-sharing-is-not-the-eucharist.

argues that, because a gathering of people happens online, it is not a proper "gathering." It could follow, then, that Christians who gather to celebrate the sacraments are united by physicality rather than faith. Third, Tilby assumes a particular theology of what is taking place when the bread is broken. The act of breaking bread "recall[s] Christ's sacrifice. This sacrificial dimension is weakened if the bread that we consume comes from the privacy of our separate kitchens." This locates God's activity, not in the faith of those partaking, but in the bread itself. Finally, she suggests that, far from being eucharistic, the eating of bread during a virtual gathering "becomes an essentially private act." She is assuming here that the symbol (in this case, bread) becomes a signifier only in the hands of the president who consecrates it.

Tilby is describing here a particular form of episcopalian sacramental praxis:

- Which is representative of a *tradition* with "recognized bounds" and rules that should never be broken. If a sacrament is celebrated without regard to these it is considered invalid.

- For Tilby, the "moment of grace," experienced as an encounter with the *covenant* God, happens within these "bounds." Furthermore she locates the authority and activity of God, the Holy Spirit, with the presidency of an ordained priest, and in the *symbol* itself.

- Even during this particular set of circumstances (a pandemic and consequent lockdown), there is rigidity of theology so that, in Tilby's view, the rules must stand, regardless of *context*. A gathering of Christians virtually cannot constitute the "body of Christ."

- It is within these structured boundaries that Tilby and her fellow Episcopalians find sacramental meaning and their *identity* as Christians.

Such sacramental theology and practice is both a product and a reflection of "centered-Christendom," and is workable for "decentered-Christendom." It assumes that there is only one acceptable means of celebrating the sacraments, and is an outworking of a hierarchical ecclesiology representative of Christendom "imaginings." Such a strong expression of Anglican Christendom-oriented theology questions the validity of other dissenting theological viewpoints. But is such a prescriptive understanding still relevant for those coming to faith within a "recentered" or "post-" Christendom society, particularly one where a lockdown of the national population is in place? Do the benefits of historical authority and the strict bounds of what is "allowed" outweigh the need for a set of sacramental practices which can be meaningful today, to Christians and non-Christians alike?

Post-Christendom and the "New Normal"

As chapter 12 revealed, there can never be a "one size fits all" definition of "what constitutes a sacrament," or indeed sacramental practice, for different ecclesial groups. As we said in our first chapter, we have sought to clarify and analyze why sacraments became regarded as such *and*, despite the fluidity of both the present time and the future, we have attempted to provide a framework for the sacramentology debate that *must* now occur, as the previous section demonstrates.

Already, as we write during the pandemic, UK magazines and newspapers contain speculative articles about what the post-COVID-19 "new normal" will look like. Of course, the church must become actively committed to the outworking of that "new normal." While we are advocating a new and ecumenical debate about sacraments, this must not become introspective, pulling the church away from the *missio Dei* in our wider communities and forums. How can the post-COVID-19, post-Christendom church ensure that its sacramental theology be made apparent to both believer and non-believer?

There are questions which must be posed:

- Do we have a eucharistic table closed to those who are seeking, or should we consider the sacraments as having evangelistic elements in their own right?

- How easily do we speak of lifelong partnership/commitment in a world that has experienced pandemic, and to what extent are committed long-term relationships, whether the result of a "marriage ceremony" or not, to be understood to be "sacramental"?

- To what extent is it possible that practices adopted by Christian communities, specifically within their own contexts, can be recognized and regarded as "sacramental" in their own right?

- How can we graciously hold an ecumenical debate about sacraments that will mean challenging the sincerely held traditional views of some of our sisters and brothers?

- Will we dare to wash the feet of all comers (even if that is only an ordinance for some)?

There are also some major theological questions to be answered, as we within the church grapple with bringing the gospel message to a population for whom the Christendom metanarrative is no longer present.

- We have spoken at length about the principle of anamnesis. If the post-Christendom church expects the sacraments to continue that function, how should it best be passed on?

- When do we teach that we are baptized into the death of Christ as his followers, or share a common Communion cup with the understanding of the radical nature of its inclusivity, without bringing into question our sensitivity to the current medical crisis?

- To what extent will the church's credibility be challenged by those who have sought but not found a place to pray or find comfort in their bereavement while many church buildings were locked to all comers, and how do we teach that the church is the people, not the walls of an empty building?

- How will the church respond to those who find faith in a "virtual" world, and for whom the term "body of Christ" requires neither physicality nor actuality? When we say, during the eucharistic prayer, that our desire is to "be one with all Christ's people," how do we explain that it really only applies to those physically present, not those they can see on Zoom or Facebook Live?

The Christian faith is one of pilgrimage and purpose. Its ultimate aim is to mediate God's plan to redeem the world, to bring reconciliation among its people, and to bring to bear a new reality in which God's reign is absolute. In setting it within this context, the immense import and possibility of sacramental praxis becomes clear. The huge significance of the oft-used phrase describing the "outward sign of an inward grace" is magnified when put into this context. We celebrate sacraments, not just as individuals wishing to commune with God, but as those thirsting to experience the salvation that has been promised to us. Through water, bread, wine, oil, and words, we are incorporated into the people of God, which is more than simply knowing—it is presence. We are re-membered as the "body of Christ." As Christians, we experience in our hearts what we know in our heads: that Christ died to save us and, in his resurrected and ascended form, he walks alongside us in order to redeem the gritty messiness of our everyday lives.

Post-Christendom begs us to allow God to hold the mirror up to ourselves and ask what we really believe, not just what our churches tell us we should believe. We can then ask ourselves how our everyday discipleship reflects this, and what place the sacraments hold for each of us as we reach God's table with outstretched hands.

COVID-19 brings our attitudes, beliefs, and practice, as well as the after Christendom debate, into even sharper relief than before. It requires us to find the answer to the question: what will be our "new normal"?

14

Conclusion

The writing of this book has been a journey of discovery for both writers, not least because the need for this book has been questioned, and the result has not been what either of us first anticipated! Readers expecting a synopsis of the question about the nature or number of sacraments potentially will reach the end of this book disappointed. However, there are plenty of other books written through the centuries dealing with that question, and there is little need for another. Many are still being written from their writers' denominational standpoints, often creating further defensive polemic for a particular traditional position.

However, there has been a paucity of works which go beyond the who, what, when, where, and how of sacramental praxis, to focus on the "why" and the "how best." While there are writers and practitioners who cling to their traditions and defend them with a self-imposed sense of persecution, there are others opening up a new level of debate surrounding the meaning of the human-divine encounter as expressed through the worship life of the church.[1] *The Oxford Handbook of Sacramental Theology*,[2] published in 2015, is a rich ground of deep thought, extending and stretching traditional sacramental understandings, while paying huge respect to the forebears of Christian tradition, whose faithfulness to their calling has resulted in a luxuriant tapestry of sacramental praxis and equivalent human-divine encounter across the globe.

At the outset of this book, we stated that we would need to deal with the issues of identity, context, and tradition. But ultimately this book is about human-divine encounter and the resultant understandings of how Christians

---

1. We would contrast the writings of Davison and Larson-Miller, to which we have previously referred, as an example of this diversity.

2. Boersma and Levering, eds., *Oxford Handbook of Sacramental Theology*.

relate to and with a covenant God. The biblical narrative shows the unfolding and evolving relationship between God and humanity which that covenant creates. We have consistently employed the phrase "human-divine" encounter, recognizing its ambiguity (as well as the need for its own book to explore that fully). Our preference for using "human-divine" in that order is drawn from Arminian[3] theology, so typical of Anglicans/Episcopalians, Methodists, and many other "children of the Reformation."[4] As COVID-19, "after Christendom," and postmodern influences coincide to alter society dramatically, the increasing number of those seeking "spiritual experience" over formalized religious habit informs our choice of the phrase "human-divine." We should not be surprised if the post-scriptural covenant relationship between God and humanity continues to unfold and evolve.

In these pages, we have sought to show how sacraments have given identity to that covenant relationship, enriching the context of the church's role and mission, while creating sufficient tradition and witness to that ongoing human-divine encounter. But we have also recognized that the unfolding and evolving relationship of that covenant means that there will *not* always be universal agreement. For example:

- There has been no time in church history when all Christians have been able to agree what a "sacrament" is, or even how many there should be; while there are other traditions that have, throughout their history, been able to live entirely without them. But sacraments do exist.

- Belief in the power of the Holy Spirit, God's empowerment in the world, unites orthodox Christians across the globe; yet the form she takes, how she manifests herself, and even the words used to describe the Spirit can be a cause for division. Belief in God's Spirit is vital.

The purpose of this book has never been to diagnose the demise or renewal of the inherited church but to recognize that advancing post-Christendom challenges affect both inherited traditions and the "new kids on the block." It is clear to us that the overriding sacramental question after Christendom is not whether sacraments exist or how many there are, but how the church, as the people of God, set within this time, in this place, facilitates the people of this time and this place to encounter a God who loves them and wants them to become agents of transformation in the world.

---

3. Arminius (1560–1609) was a Dutch theologian who countered Calvin's "double predestination" (in which God destines both who is to be saved and who is to be damned) views, assuming that Christians are "justified" by their faith and by that grace choose to open themselves up to the revelation of God.

4. Verduin, *Reformers and Their Stepchildren*.

After setting out the parameters for this book and clarifying our terms, we began by tracing the development of sacramental activity through Scripture and church history. We found that "human-divine encounter" as a concept has existed for as long as people have inhabited the earth, and that, through time, this became formalized through the development of rituals, each with its own commonly understood purpose, shared liturgy, and signifier. Those rituals, liturgies, and signifiers in turn played a role in shaping the individual and corporate identities of those participating. At the same time we noted other activities, commonly practiced, which act as conduits of human-divine experience, not recognized as "sacraments," but which might be described as "sacramental acts."

For Christians there is a distinct understanding that, during the celebration of the sacraments, Christ becomes present through the activity of the Holy Spirit.[5] While the differing traditions, contexts, and religious identities of those present result in a variety of interpretations of how this becomes so, this is a common belief and experience. In writing this book we have discovered that the way one understands the sacraments depends, in part, upon on one's pneumatology—that is, how one believes God acts in the world through the Holy Spirit. This proposition has been writ large in a way not previously imagined, through the myriad online debates between theologians and practitioners regarding the celebration of the Eucharist during the COVID-19 lockdown. Issues concerning whether the community as the "body of Christ" is truly gathered when it comes together over the internet is, in part, about how the Holy Spirit functions, and about how Christ is made present through the administration of, or immersion in, water; the sharing of bread and wine; the laying on of hands; and words of reconciliation (with or without anointing with oil).

Through the remembering of the history of the people of God, participants are themselves re-membered, becoming inheritors of a tradition reaching back as far as the beginning of creation, and anticipating its fulfillment in the age to come. Through the use of *kerygma, leiturgia,* and *diakonia,* corporate and personal identity, context, and tradition combine in a single act to open participants up to a human-divine encounter with a covenant God. We would like to suggest that it is this combination which makes an activity recognizably a "sacrament," rather than simply a "sacramental act." The label given (sacrament, ordinance, or simply a recognized activity of the church community) is far less important than the intention, which is to enable believers to experience the presence of God in Christ for themselves through the power of the Holy Spirit.

5. Baillie, *Theology of the Sacraments.*

As the modern period comes to a grinding close, and glimpses of a new epoch begin to emerge, those engaged in church after Christendom are having to come to terms with how the traditions they carry might need to be incorporated into an altered context, one where previous shared understandings of what it is to be community, and associated personal and corporate identities, are no longer fixed. In a time of such flux it might be argued that anamnesis—the re-membering so fundamental to the identity of our Christian and Abrahamic forebears—takes on a new relevance in this post-Christendom age.

Our plea is for recognition and respect for traditions that have utilized the human-divine encounter in sacraments to enrich the catholicity of their mission; but it is also necessary to recognize the ongoing work of the Spirit in those and other holy encounters, which is creating fresh apostolicity in new ways. "Behold, I do a new thing" (Isa 43:19; Jer 31:22) was not just God's intention in the time of the Hebrew prophets nor just at the post-resurrection Pentecost, but in each pivotal moment of the history of the church, including this time of "after Christendom."

Those whose current Christian identity is set within a church tradition, may well find most assurance in some of the practices associated with such traditions: Western monasticism, Franciscan spirituality, the radical Reformers' ways or today's Pentecostalism, for example. However, in the West, some of these traditions are waning and the risk is that, with the decline of formal religion and the religiosity that accompanies it, knowledge of the very fact of a loving, living, transforming God might be lost. Spirituality becomes less about building Christian community as a force for hope, and more a case of personal gratification. We might suggest that, in the face of such a reality, there is an urgent need for a reframing of sacramental theology and practice, so that it ceases to be a force of division and animosity, and becomes instead an activity that, in the words of the Apostle Paul, "builds up" the church, the body of Christ (1 Cor 10:23).

Many Christians in the early church, from later catholic traditions, and from contemporary radical or "emerging" churches have drawn from the deep well of what Alan Kreider describes as "on the Eighth Day" theology and spirituality.[6] After six days of creative fervor, God rested, giving rise to the Sabbath tradition of rest and reflection; but on the next day—Sunday (the eighth day)—it was time to begin again: "Let God begin work within us, afresh!" Nowhere is this more true than in our Easter Day celebration, on the eighth day of Holy Week, when we are re-membered in baptism and Eucharist with the Risen Lord. Such "Eighth Day" theology needs to be voiced in the

---

6. Daniélou, "La Theologie du Dimanche."

Bibliography

Anciaux, Paul. *The Sacrament of Penance*. Tenbury Wells, UK: Challoner, 1962.

Anderson, R. S., ed. *Theological Foundations for Ministry*. Edinburgh: T. & T. Clark, 1979.

Armstrong, Allan A. *The Order of Dionysis and Paul: A Brief and Historical Overview*. Bristol: ODP/Imagier, 2018.

Avvakumov, Yury P. "Sacramental Ritual in Byzantine Theology." In *The Oxford Handbook of Sacramental Theology,* edited by H. Boersma and M. Levering, 249–66. Oxford: Oxford University Press, 2015.

Baillie, D. M. *The Theology of the Sacraments (and Other Papers)*. London: Faber & Faber, 1957.

Banks, Robert. *Going to Church in the First Century*. Beaumont, TX: Christian Books, 1980.

Banks, Robert, and Julia Banks. *The Church Comes Home: Building Community and Mission through Home Churches*. 2d ed. Peabody, MA: Hendrickson, 1998.

Baring-Gould, Sabine. *Ecclesiastica Celtica*. Bristol: Imagier, 2014.

Beasley-Murray, Paul, ed. *Anyone for Ordination*. Tunbridge Wells, UK: Monarch, 1993.

Bell, Catherine. *Ritual: Perspectives and Dimensions*. Rev. ed. New York: Oxford University Press, 2009.

Berger, Peter. *Sacred Canopy: Elements of a Sociological Theory of Religion*. 2d ed. New York: Anchor, 1990.

Berlin, Adele, and Maxine Grossman, eds. "Cleanliness." *Oxford Dictionary of Jewish Religion*, 174. New York: Oxford University Press, 2011.

Boersma, Hans, and Matthew Levering, eds. *The Oxford Handbook of Sacramental Theology*. Oxford: Oxford University Press, 2015.

Boff, Leonardo. *Holy Trinity, Perfect Community*. Maryknoll, NY: Orbis, 2000.

Boff, Leonardo, and Clodovis Boff. *Introducing Liberation Theology*. Maryknoll, NY: Orbis, 1987.

Boyarin, Daniel. *Dying for God*. Redwood City, CA: Stanford University Press, 1999.

Bradbury, John. *Perpetually Reforming*. London: Bloomsbury/T. & T. Clark, 2014.

Brown, Callum G. *The Death of Christian Britain: Understanding Secularisation 1800–2000*. London: Routledge, 2001.

Brown, David. *God and the Enchantment of Place*. New York: Oxford University Press, 2004/6.

Brown, Peter. *The Rise of Western Christendom (200–1000 AD)*. Oxford: Wiley-Blackwell, 1997.

Brown, Raymond E. *The Community of the Beloved Disciple*. New York: Paulist, 1979.

Bruce, F. F. *Commentary on the Book of Acts*. London: Marshall, Morgan & Scott, 1972.

Bruce, Steve. *God is Dead: Secularization in the West*. Oxford, Blackwell, 2002.

Burke, J. Peter, and Jane E. Stets. *Identity Theory*. Oxford: Oxford University Press, 2009.

Butcher, Brian. "Orthodox Sacramental Theology." In *The Oxford Handbook of Sacramental Theology*, edited by H. Boersma and M. Levering, 329–47. Oxford: Oxford University Press, 2015.

Carter, Craig. *Re-thinking Christ and Culture: A Post-Christendom Perspective*. Grand Rapids: Brazos, 2006.

Chauvet, Louis Marie. *The Sacraments: The Word of God at the Mercy of the Body*. Collegeville, MN: Liturgical, 2001.

———. *Symbol and Sacrament: A Sacramental Re-interpretation of Christian Existence*. Collegeville, MN: Liturgical, 1995.

Church of England. *Cathedral Statistics 2018*. https://www.churchofengland.org/sites/default/files/2019-11/Cathedral%20Statistics%202018.pdf.

Claiborne, Shane. *The Irresistible Revolution*. Grand Rapids: Zondervan, 2006.

Clarke, Matthew C. *Scattering Church: Effective Mission in a Post-Institutional World*. Newcastle, AU: Turning Teardrops into Joy, 2019.

Couratin, A. H. "The Pre-history of the Liturgy." In *The Pelican Guide to Modern Theology*, edited by J. Daniélou, A. H. Couratin, and John Kent, 2, 141–56. London: Penguin, 1969.

Crossan, John Dominic. *Jesus: A Revolutionary Biography*. San Francisco, CA: Harper, 1994.

Cullmann, Oscar. *Baptism in the New Testament*. London: SCM, 1950.

———. *The Johannine Circle*. London: SCM, 1975.

Cuming, G. J., ed. *The Apostolic Tradition of Hippolytus*. Nottingham: Grove Liturgical Studies, 1991.

Daise, Michael, and James H. Charlesworth, eds. *Light in a Spotless Mirror: Reflections on Wisdom Traditions in Judaism and Early Christianity*. New York: Continuum, 2003.

Dandelion, Pink. *The Quakers: A Very Short Introduction*. Oxford: Oxford University Press, 2008.

Daniélou, J. "La Theologie du Dimanche." In *Le Jour du Seigneur*, 120–22. Out of print; revised edition published in English as *The Lord of History*, London: Longmans, 1958.

Davie, Grace. *Religion in Britain Since 1945*. Oxford: Wiley Blackwell, 2015.

Davies, Douglas. "Christianity." In *Sacred Place*, edited by Jean Holm and John Bowker, 33–61. London: Pinter/Cassell, 1994.

Davison, Andrew. *Why Sacraments?* London: SPCK, 2013.

Dawkins, Richard. *The God Delusion*. London: Black Swan, 2006.

Day, Dorothy. *Little By Little: The Selected Writings of Dorothy Day*. Edited by Robert Ellsberg. New York: Alfred A. Knopf, 1983.

de Waal, Frans. *The Bonobo and the Atheist: In Search of Humanism among the Primates*. New York: W. W. Norton, 2014.

Dix, Gregory. *The Shape of the Liturgy*. London: A. & C. Black, 1978.

Dominian, Jack. *Marriage, Faith and Love*. London: Darton, Longman & Todd, 1981.

Donovan, Vincent. *Christianity Rediscovered*. London: SCM Classics, 2001.

Duffy, Eamon. *The Stripping of the Altars: Traditional Religion in England 1400–1580*. New Haven, CT: Yale University Press, 2005.

Dulles, Avery. *Models of the Church*. New York: Doubleday/Image, 2002.

Dunn, James D. G. *The Acts of the Apostles.* London: Epworth, 1996.

———. *Unity and Diversity in New Testament.* London: SCM, 1977.

Durber, Susan, ed. *As Man and Woman Made: Theological Reflections on Marriage.* London: United Reformed Church, 1994.

Durnbaugh, Donald. *The Believers' Church: History and Character of Radical Protestantism.* Scottdale, PA: Herald, 1987.

Dyck, Cornelius J., ed. *The Classic Writings of Dirk Phillips.* Robertsbridge, UK: Plough, 2019.

Eagleton, Terry. *The Illusions of Post-Modernism.* Oxford: Blackwells, 1996.

Eco, Umberto. *The Name of the Rose.* London: Pan-Picador, 1984.

Ellsberg, Robert, ed. *Little By Little: The Selected Writings of Dorothy Day.* New York: Alfred A. Knopf, 1983.

Engel, James F., and Wilbert Norton. *What's Gone Wrong with the Harvest? A Communication Strategy for the Church and World Evangelization.* New York: Zondervan, 1975.

Faith Survey. "Christianity in the UK." 2020. https://faithsurvey.co.uk/uk-christianity.html.

Ferguson, Everett. "Sacraments in the Pre-Nicene Period." In *The Oxford Handbook of Sacramental Theology,* edited by H. Boersma and M. Levering, 125–39. Oxford: Oxford University Press, 2015.

Ferguson, Ron. *George MacLeod: Founder of the Iona Community.* Glasgow: Collins, 1990.

Fowler, James. *Stages of Faith.* New York: Bravo, 1995.

Francis, Andrew. *Anabaptism: Radical Christianity.* Bristol: Imagier/Antioch, 2010.

———. *Eat, Pray, Tell: A Relational Approach to 21st-Century Mission.* Abingdon, UK: Bible Reading Fellowship, 2018.

———. *Hospitality and Community after Christendom.* Carlisle, UK: Paternoster, 2012.

———. *Shalom—The Jesus Manifesto: Radical Theology for Our Times.* Milton Keynes: Paternoster, 2016.

———. *Spirituality and the Land.* Bristol: Imagier, forthcoming.

Gibbs, Eddie, and Ryan K. Bolger. *Emerging Churches.* Grand Rapids: Baker Academic, 2005.

Glasson, Barbara. *Mixed-up Blessing: A New Encounter with Being Church.* London: Inspire, 2006.

Gray, James, ed. *Studies in Baptism.* Birmingham: Berean, 1959.

Green, Robin. *Only Connect.* London: Darton, Longman & Todd, 1987.

Guder, Darrell, ed. *Missional Church: A Vision for the Sending Church.* Grand Rapids: Eerdmans, 1998.

Gutierrez, Gustavo. "The Option for the Poor." In *Systematic Theology: Perspectives from Liberation Theology,* edited by Jon Sobrino and Ignacio Ellacuria, 22–37. London: SCM, 1996.

Harari, Noah Yuval. *21 Lessons for the 21st Century.* London: Vintage, 2018.

———. *Homo Deus: A Brief History of Tomorrow.* London: Vintage, 2017.

———. *Sapiens: A Brief History of Humankind.* London: Vintage, 2015.

Harvey, Nicholas Peter. *Death's Gifts.* London: Epworth, 1985.

Haugaard, William P. *Elizabeth and the English Reformation.* Cambridge: Cambridge University Press, 1968.

Heathershaw, John. *Security after Christendom.* Eugene, OR: Cascade, forthcoming.

Heelas, Paul, and Linda Woodhead. *The Spiritual Revolution: Why Religion is Giving Way to Spirituality*. Oxford: Blackwell, 2004.

Higgins, A. J. B. *The Lord's Supper in the New Testament*. London, SCM, 1952.

Hirsch, Alan, and Michael Frost. *The Shaping of Things to Come: Innovation and Mission in the 21st-century Church*. Grand Rapids: Baker, 2003.

Holm, Jean, and John Bowker, eds. *Sacred Place*. London: Pinter/Cassell, 1994.

Hughes, Bettany. *Istanbul: The Tale of Three Cities*. London: Wiedenfield & Nicolson, 2017.

Hut, Hans. "The Mystery of Baptism." In *Anabaptism in Outline*, edited by Walter Klaassen, 162–89. Scottdale, PA: Herald, 1981.

Huxley, Aldous. *The Devils of Loudun*. London: Penguin, 1952.

Inge, John. *A Christian Theology of Place*. London: Routledge, 2003.

Israel, Martin. *Healing as Sacrament*. London: Darton, Longman & Todd, 1984.

Janzen, David, ed. *Fire, Salt and Peace*. Evanston, IL: Shalom Christian Communities, 1996.

Jeremias, Joachim. *The Eucharistic Words of Jesus*. London: SCM, 1977.

———. *New Testament Theology*. London: SCM, 1971.

Jones, Cheslyn, Geoffrey Wainwright, Edwin Yarnold, and Paul Bradshaw, eds. *The Study of Liturgy*. London: SPCK, 1991.

Knowles, David. *The Religious Orders of England*. 3 vols. Cambridge: Cambridge University Press, 1948, 1955, 1959.

Krahn, Cornelius. *Dutch Anabaptism*. The Hague: Martin Nijhoff, 1968.

Kreider, Alan. *The Change of Conversion and the Origin of Christendom*. Philadelphia: Trinity, 1999.

———. *English Chantries: The Road to Dissolution*. Eugene, OR: Wipf & Stock, 2012.

———. *The Patient Ferment of the Early Church*. Grand Rapids: Baker Academic, 2016.

Kreider, Alan, and Eleanor Kreider. *Worship and Mission after Christendom*. Milton Keynes: Paternoster, 2009.

Kreider, Eleanor. *Communion Shapes Character*. Scottdale, PA: Herald, 1997.

Larson-Miller, Lizette. *Sacramentality Revisited*. Collegeville, MN: Liturgical, 2016.

Lau, Franz, and Ernst Bizer. *A History of the Reformation in Germany*. London: A. & C. Black, 1964.

Lockley, Andrew. *Christian Communes*. London: SCM, 1976.

MacLeod, George, ed. *Rebuilding the Common Life*. Glasgow: Wild Goose, 1988.

Magana, Alvaro Quiroz. "Ecclesiology in the Theology of Liberation." In *Systematic Theology: Perspectives from Liberation Theology* edited by Jon Sobrino and Ignacio Ellacuria, 178–93. London: SCM, 1996.

Marshall, I. Howard. *Acts*. Grand Rapids: Eerdmans, 1980.

Martin, David. *Forgotten Revolution: Pentecostalists in Latin America*. London: SPCK, 1995.

McCreary, Alf. *In War and Peace: The Story of the Corrymeela Community*. Belfast: Brehon, 2007.

McGowan, Andrew. "A Missing Sacrament? Foot-washing, Gender, and Space in Early Christianity." *Archiv für Religionsgeschichte* 18–19 (2017) 105–22.

McGowan, Andrew B. *Ancient Christian Worship: Practices in Social, Historical, and Theological Perspective*. Grand Rapids: Baker, 2014.

McKnight, Scot. *Reading Romans Backwards*. London: SCM, 2019.

Methodist Church. *The Methodist Service Book*. London: Methodist, 1975.

Moberly, R. W. L. "Sacramentality and the Old Testament." In *The Oxford Handbook of Sacramental Theology*, edited by H. Boersma and M. Levering, 7–21. Oxford: Oxford University Press, 2015.

Moore, Charles E. *Called to Community: The Life That Jesus Wants for His People.* Robertsbridge, UK: Plough, 2016.

Moore, Peter, ed. *Man, Woman and Priesthood.* London: SPCK, 1978.

Moule, C. F. D. *The Holy Spirit.* Eugene, OR: Wipf & Stock, 1997.

Murray, Stuart. *The Naked Anabaptist.* Scottdale, PA: Herald, 2010.

Myers, Ched. *Binding the Strong Man.* Maryknoll, NY: Orbis, 2003.

Nichols, J. Randall. *Ending Marriage, Keeping Faith.* Eugene, OR: Wipf & Stock, 2002.

O'Loughlin, Thomas. *Washing Feet: Imitating the Example of Jesus in the Liturgy Today.* Collegeville, MN: Liturgical, 2015.

Otto, Rudolf. *The Idea of the Holy.* Oxford: Oxford University Press, 1976.

Peck, M. Scott. *A Different Drum: Community-making and Peace.* London: Arrow, 1990.

Pieris, Aloysius. *An Asian Theology of Liberation.* Maryknoll, NY: Orbis, 1988.

Pieterson, Lloyd. "Footwashing: Symbol, Sacrament or Subversive Ritual." https://anabaptismtoday.co.uk/index.php/home/article/view/6/18.

———. *Reading the Bible after Christendom.* Carlisle: Paternoster, 2011.

Rausch, Thomas P. *Towards a Truly Catholic Church: An Ecclesiology for the Third Millennium.* Collegeville, MN: Liturgical, 2005.

Rempel, John D. *Recapturing an Enchanted World: Ritual and Sacrament in the Free Church Tradition.* Downers Grove, IL: InterVarsity, 2020.

Robinson, William. *The Shattered Cross: The Many and the One Church.* Birmingham: Berean, 1962.

Sahi, Jyoti. "Sacred Space and Image as Sacrament." In *Gestures of God,* edited by Geoffrey Rowell and Christine Hall, 127–44. London: Continuum, 2004.

Santa, Thomas M. *Essential Catholic Handbook of Sacraments.* Ligouri, MO: Redemption, 2001.

Santos, Jose Brian. *A Community Called Taizé.* Downers Grove, IL: InterVarsity, 2008.

Saxby, Trevor J. *Pilgrims of a Common Life.* Scottdale, PA: Herald, 1987.

Scharper, Philip, and Sally Scharper. *The Gospel in Art by the Peasants of Solentiname.* Maryknoll, NY: Orbis, 1984.

Schmemann, Alexander. *Of Water and the Spirit.* Crestwood, NY: St Valdimir's Seminary, Press, 1974.

Smith, Dennis E., and Hal Taussig. *Many Tables: The Eucharist in the New Testament and Liturgy Today.* London: SCM, 1990.

Snyder, C. Arnold. *Anabaptist History and Theology: An Introduction.* Kitchener, ON: Pandora, 1995.

Sobrino, Jon. *Christology at the Crossroads.* London: SCM, 1978.

———. "The Reign of God in Liberation Theology." In *Systematic Theology: Perspectives from Liberation Theology,* edited by Jon Sobrino and Ignacio Ellacuria, 45–74. London: SCM, 1996.

Southern, R. W. *Western Society and the Church of the Middle Ages.* London: Penguin, 1978.

Stoffer, Dale. *The Lord's Supper: Believers' Church Perspectives.* Scottdale, PA: Herald, 1997.

Stutzmann, Paul Fike. *Recovering the Love Feast: Broadening Our Eucharistic Expectations.* Eugene, OR: Wipf & Stock, 2011.

Taussig, Hal. *In the Beginning was the Meal: Social Experimentation and Early Christian Identity.* Minneapolis: Augsburg Fortress, 2009.

Taylor, Daniel. *In Search of Sacred Places.* St. Paul, MN: Bog Walk, 2005.

Thomas, J. C. *Footwashing in John 13 and the Johannine Community.* Sheffield: Sheffield Academic Press, 1991.

Thompson, David M., ed. *Stating the Gospel: Formulations and Declarations of Faith from the Heritage of the United Reformed Church.* Edinburgh: T. & T. Clark, 1999.

Thurian, Max. *Confession.* Oxford: Mowbray, 1985.

———. *Priesthood and Ministry.* Oxford: Mowbray, 1983.

Tilby, Angela, "Virtual Bread Sharing is not the Eucharist." In *Church Times*, April 24 2020. https://www.churchtimes.co.uk/articles/2020/24-april/comment/columnists/angela-tilby-virtual-bread-sharing-is-not-the-eucharist.

United Reformed Church. "Baptism of Children." In *A Service Book*, 31–36. Oxford: Oxford University Press, 1990.

Verduin, Leonard. *The Reformers and Their Stepchildren.* Harrisonburg, VA: Christian Hymnary, 1990.

Walker, Andrew. *Restoring the Kingdom: The Radical Christianity of the House Church Movement.* Guildford, UK: Eagle, 1998.

Walters, William C. *Notes on the Sign or Sacrament of Holy Baptism.* London: Leopold Classics, 2015.

Westerhoff, John H. *Will Our Children Have Faith?* New York: Morehouse, 2012.

Whitaker, E. C. "Milan." In *Documents of the Baptismal Liturgy*, chapter 8. London: SCM, 1977.

Wilson, Alan. *More Perfect Union? Understanding Same-Sex Marriage.* London: Darton, Longman & Todd, 2014.

Wright, N. T. *The New Testament and the People of God.* London: SPCK, 1991.

Yoder, John Howard. *Body Politics.* Nashville: Discipleship Resources, 1997.

Printed in Great Britain
by Amazon

59322514R00091